2008: What Really Happened

Understanding the Great Financial Crisis

Todd Sheets

Encounter
BOOKS

New York • London

First American edition published in 2024 by Encounter Books,
an activity of Encounter for Culture and Education, Inc.,
a nonprofit, tax-exempt corporation.
Encounter Books website address: www.encounterbooks.com

Manufactured in the United States and printed on
acid-free paper. The paper used in this publication meets
the minimum requirements of ANSI/NISO Z39.48-1992
(R 1997) (*Permanence of Paper*).

FIRST AMERICAN EDITION

LIBRARY OF CONGRESS CATALOGING-IN-PUBLICATION DATA
IS AVAILABLE

Information for this title can be found at the Library of Congress
website under the following ISBN 978-1-64177-393-5 and LCCN 2024035338.

CONTENTS

TABLES

Part V   The Financial Crisis

Part VI   Investment Banks, Money Market Funds, and Alternative Theories of the Crisis

PREFACE

After winning the Elijah Watt Sells award on the 1981 CPA examination, I went to work in the Kansas City office of Arthur Andersen & Co. At that time, AA & Co., as we often referred to it, was the largest accounting firm in the world, with an impeccable reputation for integrity—a reputation that Andersen's Houston office would later squander in a way that played a small role in the Financial Crisis of 2008.

After a few years at AA & Co., I transitioned to investment banking, where I eventually founded and served as managing director of Raymond James Financial's REIT (real estate investment trust) investment banking practice. While at Raymond James, my fascination with investments and how they fit into and are influenced by broader macroeconomic trends led to three key insights that drove the course of my career, and, eventually, led to this book.

Sensing the opportunities created by the mid-1980s collapse of the oil-patch economy, I initiated Raymond James's Recovering Markets Program to buy apartment properties in the Southwest. All of these properties were later sold at a profit, which in some cases was substantial.

Around the same time, I foresaw how the Tax Reform Act of 1986, which eliminated most of the benefits of owning real estate in private partnerships, would eventually lead to the enormous growth of publicly traded real estate investment trusts. This insight led to the creation of Raymond James's highly successful (both for our investors and for the firm) public-market real estate investment banking group, which I founded and then led throughout the 1990s.

My involvement with the publicly traded REITs contributed to a fascination with the broader public equity markets, which led to an extended period of self-guided study of investing in the common stocks of non-real-estate companies. I accumulated a small personal library on the subject, with a special section devoted to Warren Buffett's ideas about buying and holding concentrated portfolios of great companies acquired at attractive prices.

I had started off with no savings. In fact, I fondly remember a couple of dear friends in Kansas City offering to lend me money to buy a couple of extra suits before starting at Arthur Andersen. Because of the success of these various initiatives, however, by the end of the 1990s I had accumulated enough savings to go off and manage my own portfolio, with a plan to eventually found an investment management company of my own.

Fortunately, with the Internet bubble going crazy, Wall Street had lost interest in the kind of high-quality, non-technology companies Buffett's writings had convinced me to focus on. I was able to scoop up a concentrated portfolio of stocks in such companies at what I thought were bargain prices.

When the Internet bubble finally burst in 2000 and the tech-heavy Nasdaq index collapsed, the Federal Reserve flooded the system with liquidity in an effort to keep the stock market losses from tanking the broader economy. (As we will soon see, this move played a pivotal role in the housing bubble that led to the financial crisis.) As luck would have it, much of the Fed's easy money found its way into the companies I had concentrated my portfolio in. Within a short time, I had made more money investing on my own than I had saved during the prior twenty years.

Then, two new and unexpected developments came my way.

First, the rebound in the types of stocks I was focused on made it hard to find the bargains I was looking for. I was concerned that if I used my short but attractive track record to raise investor funds I wouldn't have anywhere to put the money. In addition, I had a growing concern that the Fed's cheap-money policies were destined to end badly, but had no idea how long it might take for these dynamics to play out. These concerns dampened my interest in starting an investment fund.

While trying to sort all this out, I had the epiphany that I had earned the opportunity to do something other than focus full-time on my business career. I had never before contemplated such a possibility, but, as time wore on, the idea had a surprisingly deep and powerful pull. A period of soul-searching eventually unearthed a hidden desire to try my hand at writing a novel, and after my oldest son went off to college I started down that path.

But then came the Financial Crisis of 2008 and the unprecedented series of interventions undertaken by the Federal Reserve and the Treasury in an effort to stem the panic that followed. It felt like the traditional separations between government and the economy that had long characterized our system had suddenly been rent asunder.

Because of my earlier concerns about the Fed's interventions, I was well positioned from an investment standpoint to withstand the financial crisis, but nevertheless had a sense that the macro-economic model I had grown up with had forever changed. I was confused about big-picture economic matters I had long taken for granted and realized it was time for a new self-study program, this time focused on economic history.

Here again, my timing was serendipitous: the Internet had effectively democratized information. Because of Google and Amazon, I now had access to a wealth of research and information that far surpassed even the most impressive university library. And so I embarked on an extended study of economic history that felt every bit as enthralling as my previous endeavors. Furthermore, because of the success of those prior engagements, I now had the good fortune of being completely self-reliant. I made a personal commitment to figure out what really happened, whatever the truth might be. I had no idea where the research would lead and had not even considered that it might become a writing project. I just wanted to explore a deeply buried interest in economic history and gain a better understanding of the environment I was now investing in.

Later, while discussing my research with a lifelong friend, he commented, "You have to write this up as an editorial or something!" A new creative challenge dawned: to write economic history unveiling what I had learned—or, as I like to think of it, What Really Happened, starting with the Great Financial Crisis of 2008.

PART I

INTRODUCTION

–1–

HAMILTON, JEFFERSON, AND JACKSON

Sitting back from my desk for a moment on this late summer morning in the midst of the coronavirus epidemic, it's hard to imagine it's been over a decade since the Financial Crisis of 2008. Over a decade since an investment banking firm (Lehman Brothers) that had survived the Civil War, both World Wars, the Great Depression, the social revolution of the 1960s, and the Great Inflation of the 1970s finally came to its demise in August 2008—thereby setting off one of the most dangerous financial panics in our nation's history.

To be sure, the years following Lehman's failure elicited an abundance of material on the financial crisis, including countless articles, scholarly papers, books by most of the leading participants, and even Hollywood movies featuring A-list stars. All of which begs the question: do we really need another book on the financial crisis?

The short answer to which is: Yes because, in my opinion, we still don't have a comprehensive explanation of what really happened. And, interestingly, a brief historical review reveals that a lengthy delay from an economic crisis to an understanding of what really happened tends to be the rule rather than the exception. In fact, in some cases it has taken over a century to start setting the record straight.

Take, for example, Andrew Jackson's efforts to shut down the Second Bank of the United States in the 1830s. Closing this politically privileged institution involved an epic struggle between competing ideologies and was of great historical significance. Furthermore, this struggle was also relevant to the crisis of 2008.

The Second Bank of the United States was the successor of the first Bank of the United States, which was formed under Alexander Hamilton. The bank was a prominent symbol of Hamilton's debate with Thomas Jefferson over the proper role of the federal government in the economic affairs of the young republic. Hamilton wanted to follow the British mercantilist model wherein privately owned but governmentally privileged institutions took a leading role in guiding economic affairs. Jefferson, on the other hand, was much more a believer in Adam Smith's laissez-faire ideas. He felt that the creation of politically privileged institutions like a national bank would ultimately do more harm than good.

The Second Bank of the United States, founded in 1816, was a Hamiltonian institution: a privately owned corporation endowed with special government privileges. It was not unlike the two giant government-sponsored enterprises, Fannie Mae and Freddie Mac, that would play a central role in the Financial Crisis of 2008.

Into the debate over the Second Bank came Andrew Jackson, the nation's first president born outside the so-called "Virginia dynasty." Whereas Jefferson's objections to such institutions were philosophical in nature, Jackson's reaction to the bank was more visceral. He believed, as biographer Jon Meacham put it, that the Second Bank "made loans to influence elections, paid retainers to pro-Bank lawmakers, and could control much of the economy on a whim."[1] When we get into the causes of the financial crisis, these charges will also ring true with respect to the roles played by Fannie Mae and Freddie Mac.

Returning to the Second Bank of the United States, the point here is simply that the economic period in the 1830s following Jackson's dismantling of the bank was of great interest to later historians. And yet, it would take over a century before Peter Temin, a professor of economics (and later the department head) at MIT, finally started setting the record straight.

As Mr. Temin put it in the opening to *The Jacksonian Economy*, published in 1969:

> The period is noted both for great political changes and dramatic economic fluctuations. Yet, while controversy continues to rage about the former, there appears to be an accepted interpretation of the latter that is agreed upon by all major authorities.
>
> According to this interpretation, the economic fluctuations of the 1830's and early 1840's were the direct result of Andrew Jackson's political actions.[2]

After explaining how "all major authorities" had adopted the narrative that Jackson's closing of the Second Bank led to a reckless expansion and then a panic, Temin added, "After the panic the boom collapsed, and the economy slipped into one of the worst depressions it has known."

Temin then went on, "This story is clear, logical, and unambiguous. It shows unequivocally how Jackson's political program led the economy step by step to disaster. For those who do not admire Jackson, it has provided ample reason for rejecting his policies.... [T]he conviction that Jackson's policies were highly destructive of economic stability is a major starting point for the evaluation of the Jacksonian democracy."[3]

As Temin noted, virtually all prominent historians—from Arthur M. Schlesinger Jr. to Richard Hofstadter, Bray Hammond, and others—had adopted this narrative. But, as Temin also observed, "Despite its universal acceptance, this story will not stand close scrutiny; it is negated by the extant data of the 1830's."[4]

The primary problem, according to Temin, was that the doctrine constructed by historians relied primarily on the narrative accounts of contemporary participants, including biased insiders like Nicholas Biddle, who as head of the Second Bank was Jackson's principal antagonist in the matter. Moreover, when data *was* marshaled in support of the historians' narrative, it also tended to be anecdotal and therefore not reliable as a measure of the broad trends driving the economy. As Temin put it,

> The story of the 1830's constructed from accounts of individual banks and states is seriously in error, and it can be corrected only by the use of data about the economy as a whole. Incorporated systematically into a coherent theoretical framework, the aggregate data on the 1830's enable us to discriminate between alternate hypotheses and schemes of causation. As a result, we can say that both the traditional account is invalid and that the alternate account to be presented here is supported at many points by the available data.[5]

While some later economists have challenged portions of Temin's analysis, *The Jacksonian Economy* is still regarded as the turning point in understanding what really happened in this important era as well as one of the most important economic works of the past century. The point here is that, as Temin showed, reliable accounts of important economic events cannot be built upon anecdotes and narrowly selected facts. To be taken seriously, a theory of causation must begin with relevant *aggregate* data that enables the testing of alternate hypotheses. Temin's work enabled such an analysis; the previous historical account, though almost universally accepted, did not.

As I have already suggested, what happened with respect to the 1830s is by no means an isolated case. In fact, this scenario played out again with respect to what became the dominant narrative of the Great Depression—a narrative that, interestingly, was crafted by some of the same historians whose work on the 1830s was later discredited.

Shortly after the Great Depression, the historical community developed a narrative that the stock market crash of 1929 exposed severe imbalances in the allegedly underregulated economy. According to this narrative, the Depression represented the ultimate failure of the Jeffersonian laissez-faire model. Hence what became the dominant historical narrative supported the arguments of those who believed in the need for more government regulation and Hamiltonian intervention in the private economy.

In fact, professor Temin's comments about the historians' narrative of the 1830s can be applied almost verbatim to this narrative of the 1930s: This widely accepted story of the Great Depression is clear, logical, and unambiguous. It shows unequivocally how the laissez-faire model led step by step to disaster. For those who did not admire Jefferson's economic vision, the narrative provided ample reason for rejecting it. Indeed, the conviction that such policies were highly destructive of economic stability was a major starting point for interpreting the Great Depression.

As was the case with respect to the 1830s, however, this widely accepted story of the Depression eventually faltered under the weight of more comprehensive and rigorous analyses.

In 1963, Milton Friedman and Anna Schwartz published *A Monetary History of the United States, 1867–1960*, which included a painstakingly compiled analysis of aggregate monetary data. In particular, this analysis showed that the Great Depression was *not* caused by the failure of the private economy, as historians had long alleged. Rather, Friedman and Schwartz showed how the Federal Reserve's monetary policies were the primary domestic cause of the Depression. This understanding is now so widely accepted among economists that Ben Bernanke, the Federal Reserve chairman during the 2008 financial crisis and a self-described "Depression buff," has acknowledged Friedman and Schwartz's work as the basis for publicly admitting the Fed's culpability for the worst economic downturn in our nation's history.

Then in 1992, Barry Eichengreen, a professor of economics and political science at the University of California at Berkeley, argued that international factors also played a significant role in causing the Depression. In *Golden Fetters: The Gold Standard and the Great Depression, 1919–1939*, he argued that the collapse of the international monetary system, under the weight of the unsustainable government inflations and borrowings undertaken by Europe to finance World War I, played a pivotal role in causing the Depression.

In summary, it took nearly sixty years to understand that a significant cause of the Great Depression in fact originated in the failed postwar European monetary system—the domestic consequences of which were then compounded by the disastrous policies of the Federal Reserve.

It is almost as if we were long told that the economic patient bled to death from self-inflicted wounds, when, in fact, she actually died from an ill-conceived bleeding administered by the "medical experts" of her day.

All of which brings us back to the original point: we need another book on the Financial Crisis of 2008 because a convincing explanation built upon a systematic and coherent theory that can be tested against relevant aggregate data has yet to emerge with respect to this important event. Which, taken in context, is hardly surprising; after all, it hasn't even been two decades since the crisis.

−2−

OVERVIEW OF THE FINANCIAL CRISIS

Without the housing bubble that began in the late 1990s, there would not have been a financial crisis in 2008. The bubble pushed home prices up at unprecedented and unsustainable rates, which resulted in a historic increase in mortgage debt outstanding relative to the economy. This led to systemic exposure to mortgages at what became the critical financial institutions at the heart of the crisis. These institutions spanned the regulatory spectrum, from the heavily regulated government-sponsored enterprises (the GSEs, Fannie Mae and Freddie Mac), to the major commercial banks, and to the more lightly regulated major investment banks.

Exposure to home mortgages linked these critical institutions in the minds of the money markets. A panic was possible if the money markets lost confidence in the ability of the critical financial institutions to survive a steep drop in the value of their mortgage holdings, which is exactly what happened when, after first bailing out Bear Stearns and the GSEs, the authorities then unexpectedly allowed Lehman Brothers to fail. Lehman's failure ignited fears in the money markets that other similarly exposed critical institutions might also falter, which pushed the markets into panic mode. The panic lasted until all of the critical financial institutions had been bailed out.

The first step in unraveling the financial crisis, then, is to understand the housing bubble that created the potential for such a crisis.

THE HOUSING BUBBLE

An asset bubble occurs when prices suddenly depart from underlying fundamentals in an ultimately unsustainable manner. While asset bubbles of various types have occurred through history—for example, in Internet stocks during the 1990s—there had never been a nationwide housing bubble anything like the one that precipitated the Financial Crisis of 2008. Indeed, one reason that so many participants were caught off-guard was a belief that housing markets were essentially local and regional in nature, and therefore immune to a boom and bust on a national scale.

Yale's Robert Shiller has developed a widely respected monthly index of real (inflation-adjusted) national housing prices. I have annualized Shiller's monthly data in order to track movements in housing prices prior to and during the bubble. This work reveals that, in the century preceding the housing bubble, home prices more or less tracked inflation. In other words, before the bubble, increases in real home prices were negligible.

My analysis also reveals that, beginning in 1998, housing prices suddenly departed from these long-term historical trends. Furthermore, the analysis shows that the housing bubble that developed emerged in four distinct phases, each of which is characterized by significantly differing rates of appreciation from the phase that preceded it. Reflecting these changing rates of appreciation, I have called these phases: Liftoff, Acceleration, Deceleration, and Crash. In order to set a standard of comparison, I have also constructed a Base Period consisting of the years immediately preceding the onset of the housing bubble.

Let's take a quick look at each of these phases, beginning with the Base Period.

Base Period (1994–1997): During the four years immediately preceding the onset of the bubble, real home prices *declined* by an annual average of 0.2%, which is to say that, consistent with the prior historical trend, home prices basically tracked inflation.

Liftoff (1998–2001): After declining slightly over the previous four years, real home prices suddenly began to increase at an average annual rate of 4.7% during Liftoff.

Acceleration (2002–2005): In the early 2000s, the rate of real home price appreciation shot up again, to an average annual rate of 8.3%, reaching a peak of 10.4% in 2005.

Deceleration (2006): In 2006, the rate of increase in real home prices slowed dramatically, to 3.5% for the year.

Crash (2007–2012): Beginning in 2007, real housing *prices* declined for several years, eventually falling about one-third from the bubble's peak.

Another way to appreciate the magnitude of the housing bubble is to consider the longer historical context from a slightly different perspective. I noted earlier that long-term home prices have basically tracked inflation. During the century leading up to the bubble, the cumulative increase in real housing prices was 6.5%. Then, during the nine years of the bubble, home prices rose by 71%, or *over ten times the increase in the prior one hundred years.*

One of the most prominent and enduring theories regarding the housing bubble is that it was somehow the result of a gradual deregulation of financial markets. I will later return to a number of issues with this explanation, but we can already see that this theory fails to account for the sudden liftoff of home prices in 1998 or for the dramatic changes in appreciation rates during each of the ensuing phases of the bubble.

Others have pointed to the role of Fannie Mae and Freddie Mac (the GSEs), but the idea that the bubble was *solely* caused by the GSEs fails to explain the rapid acceleration in the rate of housing appreciation in the early 2000s, when large commercial and investment banks played such a significant role in financing home purchases.

Still others have posited that the bubble was caused by the easy-money policies of the Fed in the early 2000s, but proponents of this theory have had trouble accounting for the escalation of housing prices in the late 1990s, *before* the Fed dramatically lowered interest rates.

A plausible theory of causation must explain the sudden onset and the distinct phases of the bubble. In the detailed discussions that follow, I will show that the Liftoff phase of the bubble in 1998 was triggered by the rapid expansion undertaken by Fannie Mae and Freddie Mac. Furthermore, I will show that this expansion was supply-driven, meaning that it originated with the GSEs themselves and was not merely a response by the GSEs to increased demand coming from the marketplace. Additionally, I will show that the GSEs' expansion was aided and abetted by federal housing policy.

My analysis then shows that the Acceleration phase of the bubble (2002–2007) was driven by the Federal Reserve's ultralow interest rate policies. Much of the criticism of Fed policy during this period has been based on what is known as the "Taylor rule," a widely followed barometer that considers the federal funds rate in relation to inflation and GDP. With respect to the housing bubble, however, I will show that the critical measure was not defined by the Taylor rule, but was rather a function of the relationship between short-term interest rates and housing appreciation. The core problem with the Fed's interest rate policy during this period was that, in the midst of the elevated home price appreciation triggered by the GSEs, the Fed unwittingly reduced short-term interest rates to levels that were below the rate of home price appreciation. This unprecedented circumstance caused a surge in demand for variable-rate loans, which in turn propelled the acceleration of home price appreciation in the early to mid-2000s. I will show that the expansion in the mortgage market during this phase of the bubble represented a demand-driven response to the Fed's misguided interest rate policies.

We will then see that the Deceleration and the Crash phases of the bubble were also driven by changes in Fed policy.

THE FINANCIAL CRISIS

The housing bubble pushed mortgage debt outstanding from about 44% of GDP in 1997 to 72% in 2007, which is to say that one effect of the GSEs' expansion and the Fed's interest rate policies was to push home mortgages up to a level that had an unprecedented potential to affect the entire economy. When the bubble finally imploded, housing prices dropped precipitously, which threatened the value of the mortgage assets held on the books of the critical financial institutions at the heart of the financial crisis. Providers of short-term capital worried that declining mortgage values could threaten the solvency of critical institutions. When such fears turned to panic, the financing markets froze up.

I have used movements in the S&P 500 index of large capitalization stocks and in the TED spread, a measure of stress in the short-term financing markets, to chart the course of the financial crisis. Based on this analysis, I have broken the financial crisis down into four stages:

Awareness (June 2007–October 2007): During the Awareness stage, hedge funds managed by Bear Stearns and BNP Paribas that were heavily concentrated in U.S. home mortgages announced significant write-downs of their assets. This put the markets on notice that the collapse of home prices was beginning to weigh on mortgage values. Market indicators initially dropped in reaction to the hedge fund write-downs, but then largely recovered. The S&P 500 rose by an average of 0.2% per month during this stage.

Stress (November 2007–August 2008): Beginning in the fall of 2007, a steady procession of substantial mortgage-related write-downs and losses announced by a wide swath of major financial institutions alerted the financial markets that housing-related problems were deepening and spreading. Market indicators became stressed during this period, but did not reflect panicked conditions. This state of affairs continued through the spring and early summer even as Bear Stearns and the GSEs reached the point of needing federal bailouts to survive. The S&P 500 *dropped* by an average of 1.7% per month during the Stress stage.

Panic (September 2008–February 2009): After bailing out Bear Stearns and the GSEs, the authorities then unexpectedly allowed Lehman Brothers to fail. Worried that declining mortgage values could push other firms to the point of failure and no longer confident in their ability to predict when the authorities would provide bailout financing, the markets panicked. The S&P 500 dropped by an average of 7.1% per month during this stage.

Recovery (March 2009–): The markets remained in a state of panic until bailout financing was arranged and publicly committed to each of three critical financial institutions—Citigroup, Merrill Lynch, and Bank of America. A sustained recovery in the S&P 500 began shortly after the last of these bailouts was announced in January 2009.

This timeline reveals that the panic in the markets was triggered by the uncertainty over bailout policy that followed Lehman's failure. Furthermore it shows that the resolution of the panic primarily revolved around the three critically endangered institutions: Citigroup, Merrill Lynch, and Bank of America. While the bailout-sink-like response of the authorities that followed Lehman's failure was undoubtedly of some help, the real key to resolving the panic was the resolution of money market fears regarding these three institutions. Furthermore, this timeline reveals that the stress tests conducted in the spring of 2009 were not, as some have asserted, the key to resolving the panic. The results of the tests were announced in early May 2009, by which time the markets were already recovering. The stress tests did confirm, however, that the overall state of the financial markets was generally sound and that the real source of panic primarily revolved around the resolution of fears about the three critical firms mentioned above.

This analysis also further contradicts the gradual deregulation narrative of the financial crisis. This deregulation narrative was mainly focused on the idea that the investment banks (the least heavily regulated sector of the financial markets) were largely to blame for the crisis. But failure occurred across the regulatory spectrum, from the heavily regulated GSEs and commercial banks to brokerage firms like Bear Stearns, Lehman Brothers, and Merrill Lynch. In fact, one of the critical commercial banks, Citigroup, was regulated in part by the Federal Reserve itself.

INVESTMENT BANKS, MONEY MARKET FUNDS, AND ALTERNATIVE THEORIES

THE INVESTMENT BANKS

The Fed's historic bailout of Bear Stearns and Lehman's failure were defining moments of the leadup to the Panic stage of the crisis. In the aftermath, there was an intense focus on the major investment banks—which also included Merrill Lynch, Goldman Sachs, and Morgan Stanley—and on the idea that they caused the crisis. However, as was also the case with respect to the Second Bank in the 1830s and the Depression in the 1930s, the rush to assign blame often led commentators down streets littered with memorable anecdotes, leaving more rigorous analysis and fact checking by the wayside.

To help understand what really happened, I have combined and analyzed the financial statements of the major investment banks. This analysis shows that the rate of growth for the investment banks was in the mid to upper teens during the early to mid-2000s, that the leverage employed by these institutions was high but consistent with their historical norms, and that their combined exposure to derivatives did not vary meaningfully during this period. All of which should give pause to those who believe that additional regulatory scrutiny would have identified problems missed by the management, directors, and contemporary regulators of these companies.

Why then did some of the investment banks fail while others survived? I believe the differentiating factor was the level of tangible stockholders' equity relative to mortgage assets maintained by these firms. Bear Stearns and Lehman were at the low end of this ratio. Merrill Lynch was similarly capitalized but benefited from the intangible value of its retail brokerage firm, which made it an attractive acquisition target. Goldman Sachs and Morgan Stanley each maintained significantly higher levels of tangible equity relative to their mortgage assets, which enabled them to arrange private market financings that helped make them self-sufficient.

MONEY MARKET MUTUAL FUNDS

While money market mutual funds did not cause the crisis, the panic did expose their use of stable dollar reporting as a key weakness in the regulation and operation of such funds. Unfortunately, the regulatory response to the crisis only partially resolved this flaw. I believe that stable dollar reporting should be banned for all money market funds, and that all such funds should be required to report their actual, floating, net asset values.

ALTERNATIVE THEORIES

As noted earlier, the prominent roles played by Bear Stearns and Lehman Brothers in the crisis led many to adopt the narrative that the crisis was caused by a gradual relaxation of regulatory oversight, especially with respect to the major investment banks. The analysis set forth herein shows that this narrative is inconsistent with the sudden acceleration in home prices that began in 1998 and the distinct turning points in the housing bubble thereafter. Additionally, this narrative is inconsistent with the fact that failure occurred across the regulatory spectrum, from highly regulated institutions like the GSEs and Citigroup to the less heavily regulated investment banks. Furthermore, federal housing policy changes actually encouraged the rapid expansion of the GSEs that triggered the onset of the housing bubble.

As the analysis herein shows, the Federal Reserve was directly responsible for the Acceleration phase of the bubble. Both Alan Greenspan and Ben Bernanke were not only complicit in these mistakes, but also repeatedly denied that their interest rate policies had anything to do with the bubble. Rather, they blamed the money flowing into housing on an alleged "global savings glut," an argument that the Fed itself later disavowed.

The point here is not to blame the regulators, but rather is much the same as the one made by Professor Temin of MIT with respect to the 1830s: the gradual deregulation narrative has been widely adopted and may at first blush appear to provide a plausible explanation, but it is largely constructed from anecdotes, the accounts of talented but biased insiders, and selected facts. The analysis presented herein shows that this theory is inconsistent with the aggregate data on the housing bubble and the financial crisis.

–4–

PRACTICAL LESSONS

PREVENTING A FUTURE CRISIS

Given the understanding of the housing bubble set forth herein, the keys to preventing a future crisis like that of 2008 are to:

1. Revoke the GSEs' special government privileges.
2. Eliminate or drastically curtail the ability of the Fed to inflate asset bubbles.
3. Require *all* money market mutual funds to report actual, variable, net asset values.

RISK MONITORING

One problem exposed by the crisis was that supposedly sophisticated financial risk models failed to alert executives, directors and regulators of the dangers resulting from the housing bubble and growing mortgage exposure. The analysis set forth herein suggests that corporate overseers should focus on the following guidelines:

1. Measure key areas of asset exposure against historical benchmarks for signs that bubble-like conditions might be devel-

oping. Robert Shiller's indexes for housing and the S&P 500 provide two excellent examples of readily available benchmarks. Similarly, potential risks in the value of fixed-income investments should be considered by estimating values based on historically normal interest rate environments.

2. When a significant deviation from past pricing norms develops—as was the case with housing during the bubble and has happened more recently with respect to fixed-income investments held by commercial banks—monitor the ratio of tangible stockholders' equity (TSE) relative to the exposed asset class. This ratio should be compared to historical norms for both the institution under scrutiny and its peers.

3. Consider what would happen to TSE if valuations for the exposed asset class returned to historical norms.

POLITICALLY PRIVILEGED INSTITUTIONS

One critical takeaway from the analysis presented herein reaches all the way back to the founding of the country and the argument between Alexander Hamilton and Thomas Jefferson over the creation of politically privileged institutions like the Second Bank of the United States. As you may recall, Hamilton favored such institutions and Jefferson did not. Suffice to say, the role of the GSEs in causing the Liftoff phase of the housing bubble that led to the financial crisis favors Jefferson's side of this long-running debate.

THE FEDERAL RESERVE

The discussion that follows also shows that it is incumbent upon market participants to beware of the risk of asset bubbles resulting from the Federal Reserve's interest rate manipulations. As suggested under "Risk Monitoring," one way to do this is to compare asset values to historical benchmarks. Another way to help monitor the risk of asset bubbles is to track the real federal funds rate. The period between the runaway inflation of the 1970s and the Acceleration phase of the housing bubble that began in 2002 provides a useful benchmark for the real federal funds rate during a period of relatively benign monetary policy. During this period, the real federal funds rate averaged 2.5%. When the real federal funds rate drops below this level for prolonged periods, market participants should be on heightened alert for the risk of asset bubbles.

Another key lesson that will develop from the following discussion has to do with the history of the Federal Reserve. Milton Friedman and Anna Schwartz have shown that the Fed played a major causative role in both the Great Depression of the 1930s and the Great Inflation of the 1970s. The analysis presented herein shows that the Fed also played a major role in causing the Financial Crisis of 2008. Friedman once observed of the Fed, "In one respect the System has remained completely consistent throughout. It blames all problems on external influences beyond its control and takes credit for any and all favorable occurrences. It thereby continues to propagate the myth that the private economy is unstable, while its behavior continues to document the reality that government today is the major source of economic instability."[1]

Consistent with these observations, the powers of the Fed were expanded enormously in the aftermath of the financial crisis. What then are we to make of the Fed's ever-growing powers in spite of the enormity of its many failures? Mistaken narratives are one obvious explanation. In addition, the Fed's history of helping to bail the Reagan administration out of the stock market crash of 1987, smoothing the Clinton administration's NAFTA transition in the 1990s, and bailing the Bush administration out from the collapse of the tech stock bubble in the 2000s evidences its unique ability to promote the one bipartisan interest all politicians hold dear: reelection. In other words, until we begin to hold the Fed accountable for its mistakes, it is hard to imagine how things could possibly change.

PART II

THE HOUSING BUBBLE

–5–

HAMILTON AND RAINES

Anyone who has seen the hit Broadway musical *Hamilton*, or read the book by Ron Chernow on which it is based, knows something about Alexander Hamilton's remarkable rise from his bastard childhood in the British West Indies to become an aide-de-camp to George Washington during the Revolutionary War before being appointed as the nation's first secretary of the treasury. As Mr. Chernow observed of the work ethic that would help turn the young Hamilton into an early exemplar of the American Dream: "He often worked past midnight, curled up in his blanket, then awoke at dawn and paced the nearby burial ground, mumbling to himself as he memorized his lessons. (Hamilton's lifelong habit of talking sotto voce while pacing lent him an air of either inspiration or madness.)"[1]

Earlier we saw how Hamilton's vision of an interventionist federal government patterned on the British mercantilist model contrasted with Thomas Jefferson's laissez-faire views. With the Bank of England as a model, Hamilton founded the first Bank of the United States, which became a lightning rod in the debate between the Jeffersonian and Hamiltonian ideals. That bank's successor, the Second Bank of the United States, played a significant role in the presidency of Andrew Jackson, who saw the politically privileged bank as a heinous institution that "made loans to influence elections, paid retainers to pro-Bank lawmakers, and could control much of the nation's economy on a whim."[2]

Mark Twain famously observed that history doesn't repeat, but it often rhymes. As we begin to examine the onset of the housing bubble and how it gave rise to the financial crisis that followed, you may well hear the chimes of history ringing in the background.

More than two hundred years after Alexander Hamilton's rise from the most humble of circumstances to the heights of early American power and influence, another young man would embark on a strikingly similar journey. Franklin Delano Raines grew up in the 1950s in an economically disadvantaged family in Seattle, Washington. When Franklin was still in elementary school, his working-class father became ill and lost his job, forcing the family to go on welfare. His father eventually recovered, and then took any job he could find to support his family. In a *New York Times* profile, Franklin recalled tagging along with his dad to pick beans in the fields outside of town: "You'd get picked up at 2 o'clock in the morning down on Skid Row. You'd start picking when the sun came up and you'd finish at 4. A grown man could earn $10 a day. A kid could earn $5, plus all the beans you could bring home."[3]

Like Hamilton, Franklin Raines marshaled a keen intellect and prodigious work ethic to leverage himself up from his humble beginnings. He was accepted into the upper echelons of academia, earned a BA and a law degree from Harvard, and then studied as a Rhodes Scholar at Oxford. After working in the Carter administration during the 1970s, Raines joined the distinguished investment banking firm of Lazard Freres, where he became a general partner. In the early 1990s, he transitioned into the vice chairmanship at Fannie Mae, but was tapped by Bill Clinton to head the U.S. Office of Management and Budget. Then, in 1998, Raines left the Clinton administration to become the chief executive officer of Fannie Mae.

Raines's move back to Fannie Mae coincided almost exactly with the onset of the housing bubble, which was no mere coincidence. For Raines, Fannie Mae's mission to provide home mortgage financing to low- and moderate-income families was not just a matter of public policy—it was personal. He recalled watching his father build their home with his own two hands and what this effort meant for the family: "Five years it took him. He dug the foundation by hand. He built the frame. He bought a house that the state was going to tear down for a highway and he pulled it apart for the materials. He could only build as he and my mother earned money. It was an incredible process he went through."[4]

I followed Fannie Mae as a company for a while in the late 1990s and early 2000s, and I remember listening to Mr. Raines talk about how important that home was to his family's ability to accumulate savings, and how that memory helped fire his sense of Fannie Mae's mission to help others do the same. It was clear to me then—as I still believe to this day—that Raines was not only hardworking, humble, and erudite, but also sincere in his desire to help other working-class families achieve the American Dream of owning their own home.

Nevertheless, even the most honorable intentions, implemented by talented and sincere leaders, do not ensure that Hamiltonian interventions will yield results that match their noble aspirations. As we will later see, the rapid expansion undertaken by Fannie Mae and led by Raines ultimately produced just the opposite of what was intended: a cataclysmic loss of hard-earned savings by millions of working-class homeowners who were lured by the prospect of quick wealth conjured up from a housing market that had previously worked so well for so many for so long.

–6–

PREVIEW

As was noted previously, the first step in unraveling the Financial Crisis of 2008 is to understand the housing bubble that created the potential for a crisis. The housing bubble that began in 1998 led to a historic increase in mortgage debt relative to the economy, which created systemic exposure to mortgages at what became the critical financial institutions. This linked these institutions to one another in the minds of the money markets. When one of these critical institutions (Lehman Brothers) was unexpectedly allowed to fail, the money markets panicked over the fear that other systemically exposed institutions might also be allowed to fail.

In this section we will begin by looking at historical housing prices, which will show that in both the longer period and in the shorter four-year period leading up to the bubble, housing prices basically tracked inflation. Then, in 1998, home price appreciation suddenly lifted off from its historical relationship to inflation. In 2002, another dramatic change occurred when housing prices began to accelerate even more rapidly until 2005, when the pace of real appreciation suddenly decelerated. Then, in 2006, home prices began the historic crash that led to the declining mortgage values on the books of the critical financial institutions that were systemically linked to one another in the minds of the panicking money markets.

Developing this profile of the housing bubble provides us with an objective framework, based on aggregate housing data, that will be used to test the theories of causation covered in the following sections.

HISTORICAL HOME PRICES

Robert Shiller, a Nobel Prize–winning economist at Yale, has developed a highly regarded monthly index of inflation-adjusted national housing prices. This index extends back to 1890, which enables an understanding of historical patterns in home prices prior to the onset of the housing bubble.

Before turning to the data, let's clarify the difference between real (inflation-adjusted) changes in home prices and nominal (unadjusted) changes. Suppose that the national average home price in a given year is $100,000. Let's also assume that home prices grow by 3.0% during the following year, which pushes the price of our hypothetical average home up to $103,000. If general inflation throughout the economy is also 3.0% during that year, then the inflation-adjusted value of the home at the end of the year will also be $103,000. In this scenario, *nominal* home prices have increased by 3.0%. But *real* home price appreciation, which is determined by subtracting the rate of inflation (3.0%) from the rate of nominal appreciation (3.0%), has remained flat, which is to say that the inflation-adjusted rate of home appreciation is 0.0%.

Now, let's use this example to see how inflation adjustments work in a housing index like the one that Shiller created. If the starting point for a housing index is set at 100, and if housing price increases *exactly* match inflation thereafter, then the index will also equal 100 at the end of the period under study. For example, assume we are looking at a one-year period where inflation is at 3.0% and housing prices increase at the same rate. After a year of 3.0% growth, the *nominal* housing index will have increased from 100 to 103. Because assumed general inflation is 3%, the inflation index is also at 103 at the end of the year. Consequently, the *inflation-adjusted* housing index will still be 100, the result we get by dividing the nominal housing index of 103 by the general inflation index of 103 and then multiplying by 100. *Relative to inflation*, then, housing prices at the end of this hypothetical period are the same as at the beginning.

If housing prices generally move more or less in sync with inflation over time, then we would expect that an inflation-adjusted index of housing prices would come reasonably close to performing like the index in the example above—i.e., the housing price index would be 100 at the beginning of the period and would still be pretty close to 100 at the end. In reality, various factors besides inflation affect housing prices over time, so there won't be a perfect correlation, but we would expect the ending inflation-adjusted housing index to be fairly close to its beginning point. If the index is pushed off track for a while, we would then expect it to trend back toward its starting point.

Shiller's index shows that national housing prices did indeed track inflation very closely for a century prior to the housing bubble. The raw data in Shiller's index that I used for this analysis includes annual readings from 1890 through the mid-1940s, and then monthly readings thereafter. I created annual averages out of Shiller's monthly data to determine trends in real housing prices over the long term and during the housing bubble.

The final year before the onset of the bubble was 1997. If we begin in that year and work backward in ten-year increments, we

Real Home Prices: 1897–2006   **Table II.1**

Source of underlying data: Robert J. Shiller, *Irrational Exuberance**

Year	Real Home Price Index	
1897	107	*In 1897, the index of real housing prices was at 107.*
1907	109	
1917	85	WW I
1927	71	
1937	80	The Great Depression
1947	109	*After WW II, the index returned to about where it had started.*
1957	114	
1967	106	
1977	109	*80 years later, the index was still largely unchanged.*
1987	125	LT interest rates drop precipitously in the mid-'80s.
1997	114	*Just before the bubble, real home prices were up less than 7% in 100 years.*
2006	195	*During the 9 years of the bubble, real prices rose 71%.*

*   U.S. Home Price and Related Date from *Irrational Exuberance*, 3rd edition (Princeton University Press, 2016), as updated by author

get a good idea of how inflation-adjusted home prices developed over the previous century, as is set forth in Table II.1. As this table shows, except for declines during World War I and the Great Depression, home prices essentially tracked inflation until the early 1980s: the inflation-adjusted index was at 107 in 1897, at 109 in 1947, and at 109 in 1977.

Because of the rapid decline of interest rates in the early 1980s, home prices appreciated faster than inflation until the late '80s, but then began to trend back down toward the long-term inflation-adjusted index. Over the one hundred years from 1897 to 1997, the *cumulative* increase in *real* home prices was only about 6.5%.

Then, in 1998, a sudden and dramatic departure from the historical norm occurred. Over a period of nine years (1998–2006), real home prices shot up by 71%, more than ten times the cumulative increase over the previous one hundred years.

If we asked Simon and Garfunkel about the sudden end of the predictable and reliable streak that had long characterized the national housing market before the bubble, they might have responded with something like, "Where have you gone, Joe DiMaggio?"[1]

–8–

THE PHASES OF THE BUBBLE

Now let's take a look at the years leading up to the onset of the bubble. As mentioned above, coincident with a declining interest rate cycle that started in the early 1980s, housing prices began to appreciate above the long-running relationship with inflation for a short time. We'll start with 1982 and then follow home prices until just before the bubble began to inflate.

If we trace a finger down the column headed "Real Index" in Table II.2, we find that the peak year for housing prices during this period was 1989, when the index was at 130.3. Although not reflected in the table, this was also the peak for *the entire history* of the index prior to the housing bubble.

Continuing down through the years after the peak, we see that the inflation-adjusted index then gradually declined—from 130.3 in 1989 down to 113.7 in 1997. This shows that, after a brief uptick in the 1980s, home prices trended back toward their long-term average relationship to inflation. The index in 1997 was less than 5 percent above where it had been in 1982, and about 6.5% above where it had been a century earlier.

To reiterate the key point, home prices essentially tracked inflation from the late 1890s until 1997. There were a couple of short

Real Home Prices: 1982–1997   **Table II.2**

Source of underlying data: Shiller

Year	Real Index (Avg. for Yr.)	
1982	108.6	
1983	108.4	
1984	108.8	
1985	111.2	
1986	118.7	
1987	124.8	
1988	128.7	
1989	130.3	*Prior to the housing bubble, 1989 was the highest point in the history of the index, which dates to 1890.*
1990	126.0	
1991	119.3	
1992	116.4	
1993	114.7	
1994	114.7	
1995	113.7	
1996	113.0	
1997	113.7	*In 1997, just prior to the onset of the bubble, real home prices were less than 7% above the level of a century earlier.*

aberrations, but the index then self-corrected back toward the rate of general inflation.

BASE PERIOD: 1994–1997

In order to establish a baseline for housing appreciation before things started to change so dramatically, let's focus on what I will call the Base Period, i.e., the four years immediately prior to the onset of the housing bubble.

In Table II.3, a single line is drawn above 1994 to mark the beginning of the Base Period. The "Percent Change" column shows that 1993 was the last year that the index declined by more than 1.0% as real home prices trended down from their 1989 peak and back toward the long-term average relationship to inflation. Beginning in 1994,

Real Home Prices: Base Period (1994–1997)   **Table II.3**

Source of underlying data: Shiller

Year	Real Index (Avg. for Yr.)	Pct. Chg.
1990	126.0	-3.3%
1991	119.3	-5.4%
1992	116.4	-2.4%
1993	114.7	-1.5%
1994	114.7	0.0%
1995 *Base*	113.7	-0.9%
1996 *Period*	113.0	-0.7%
1997	113.7	0.7%
Avg. Chg. for Base Period	*113.8*	*-0.2%*

Consistent with the historical trend, home prices basically tracked inflation in the 4 years immediately prior to the bubble.

home prices again started to track inflation much more closely. In fact, on average, home prices rose at a pace slightly *below* inflation for the next few years until 1997, when price increases exceeded inflation, but only by a small amount (0.7%). During the four-year Base Period as a whole, the index of real housing prices *dropped* from 114.7 to 113.7. This represents an aggregate decline of about 1%, or an average annual decline of approximately 0.2%.

LIFTOFF: 1998–2001

In 1998, the rate of real home appreciation changed suddenly and dramatically.

After lagging inflation for the first three years of the Base Period and then rising by just 0.7% in 1997, real home prices jumped by 4.0% in 1998, and the annual rate of appreciation remained at or above this elevated level throughout the four years of the Liftoff, as shown in Table II.4 below.

As this table shows, after *declining* by an annual average of 0.2% during the Base Period, real housing prices rose at an average annual rate of 4.7% during Liftoff. Clearly, something significant happened

Real Home Prices: Liftoff (1998–2001)   **Table II.4**

Source of underlying data: Shiller

Year		Real Index (Avg. for Yr.)	Pct. Chg.	
1994		114.7	0.0%	
1995	*Base*	113.7	-0.9%	
1996	*Period*	113.0	-0.7%	
1997		113.7	0.7%	
Avg. Chg. for Base Period			-0.2%	
1998		118.3	4.0%	*After tracking inflation during the Base*
1999	*Liftoff*	123.8	4.7%	*Period, home prices suddenly spiked upward in 1998...*
2000	*Phase*	130.2	5.2%	
2001		136.8	5.1%	
Avg. Chg. for Liftoff			4.7%	*...and remained elevated throughout Liftoff.*

in the housing markets in 1998 that caused a sudden departure from both the long-term norm and the shorter-term trends leading up to that point. Knowing that the bubble began so abruptly at this particular point in time reveals that something dramatic changed in the housing markets in 1998. Any plausible explanation for the housing bubble must account for this sudden change of events.

ACCELERATION: 2002–2005

Beginning in 2002, the rate of real home price appreciation began to accelerate even more rapidly than it had during Liftoff. Beginning with an increase of 6.3% in 2002, real home price appreciation continued to escalate through 2005, when it peaked at the extraordinary rate of 10.4%.

To put these annual increases in perspective, recall that in 1997 the index was only about 6.5% above its beginning point from *a century earlier*.

Table II.5 details the dramatic changes in the rate of housing appreciation from the Base Period through the Acceleration phase.

Real Home Prices: Acceleration (2002–2005)　　　　　　　　　　**Table II.5**

Source of underlying data: Shiller

Year		Real Index (Avg. for Yr.)	Pct. Chg.	
1994		114.7	0.0%	
1995	*Base*	113.7	-0.9%	
1996	*Period*	113.0	-0.7%	
1997		113.7	0.7%	
Avg. Chg. for Base Period			*-0.2%*	
1998		118.3	4.0%	
1999	*Liftoff*	123.8	4.7%	
2000	*Phase*	130.2	5.2%	
2001		136.8	5.1%	
Avg. Chg. for Lift-off Period			*4.7%*	
2002		145.4	6.3%	*In '02 appreciation picked up again, and then continued to escalate…*
2003	*Acceleration*	155.5	6.9%	
2004	*Phase*	170.4	9.6%	
2005		188.2	10.4%	*…finally reaching a peak in '05.*
Avg. Chg. for Acceleration			*8.3%*	*Average appreciation was substantially higher than during Liftoff.*

This table shows that the average annual rate of appreciation rose from *minus* 0.2% during the Base Period to 4.7% during Liftoff and then to 8.3% during the Acceleration phase.

To grasp the historic magnitude of what happened as the housing bubble took off, consider that, after rising by a cumulative 6.5% in the *century* preceding the onset of the bubble, real prices suddenly grew by 20% during the four years of the Liftoff and then by an additional 38% during the four years of Acceleration.

Again, beginning in 1998, something significant and unprecedented suddenly started to affect national housing prices, and then, in 2002, another dramatic change occurred.

DECELERATION: 2006

A bit like a car trying to keep from careening off a cliff, real home price appreciation skidded to a near standstill in 2006. The rate of appreciation had escalated rapidly through 2005 to a peak of 10.4%. Then, in the following year, real appreciation fell precipitously, to just 3.5%.

In short, in 2006 the rate of the bubble's expansion suddenly dropped by almost two-thirds.

CRASH: 2007–2012

In reference to great investments that keep on growing, Warren Buffett liked to quote the old Mae West line, "Too much of a good thing is wonderful!" With respect to the artificial elevation of the housing bubble, however, "What goes up must come down" seems a bit more appropriate.

From 1998 to 2006, an unprecedented and unsustainable bubble of vast proportions inflated over the housing landscape. During the nine years of the bubble, home prices increased ten times as much relative to inflation as they had in the previous one hundred years. Then the bubble started to deflate. From 2007 through 2012, real housing prices dropped by approximately one-third.

Many of the homeowners pulled in by the bubble's allure lost much or all of the equity they had invested in their homes. Those who owned stock in the critical financial institutions would soon see the value of their investments plummet and in some cases wiped out entirely. Many who had invested their careers in these institutions lost their jobs.

Real Home Prices: Crash (2007–2012)   Table II.6

Source of underlying data: Shiller

Years		Total Cumulative Real Appreciation	
1897–1997	Pre-bubble — 100 years	7%	*During the 9 years of the bubble, prices appreciated over 10x the level of cumulative appreciation in the 100 years before the bubble.*
1998–2006	The bubble — 9 years	71%	
2007–2012	Crash — 6 years	-33%	

–9–

SUMMARY

There had never before been anything like the housing bubble that started in 1998. At its peak in 2007, Shiller's index of real housing prices was roughly 50% higher than at any time during the previous 117 years.

The bubble emerged suddenly in 1998 and then went through a number of distinct phases, which are summarized in the following table.

Consistent with the longer-term historical trend, national home prices essentially tracked inflation during the four-year Base Period

Real Home Prices: Review   **Table II.7**

Source of underlying data: Shiller

Years	Stage		Avg. Annual Real Appreciation	
'94–'97	Base Period		-0.2%	Consistent with long-term trends, real home prices basically tracked inflation prior to the bubble.
'98–'01	Liftoff		4.7%	Beginning in 1998, home prices suddenly accelerated...
'02–'05	Acceleration	The years of the housing bubble	8.3%	...then grew even faster during Acceleration.
'06	Deceleration		3.5%	In '06 the rate of appreciation suddenly dropped.
'07–'12	Crash		-6.3%	Real home prices started falling in '07.

(1994-1997) preceding the bubble, falling by an average rate of 0.2% during these years. During Liftoff (1998–2001), real home price appreciation suddenly spiked up to an annual average of 4.7%. Then, during the Acceleration phase (2002–2005), the rate of appreciation soared to an annual average of 8.3%, roughly 75% faster than the already elevated levels of the Liftoff phase. After peaking at 10.4% in 2005, the rate of home price increases suddenly dropped sharply, to 3.5% in 2006, before falling precipitously during the Crash (2007–2012).

To help put all of this in perspective: during the one hundred years preceding the bubble, real housing prices increased by a cumulative total of 6.5%. Then, during the nine years of the bubble, home prices shot up by 71%, only to be followed by a drop of 33% during the Crash.

Whenever a development like the housing bubble suddenly appears in a market that had previously worked so well for so long, we must ask: what changed? Why, all of a sudden, did this market begin to function so differently from the long historical pattern that preceded it?

In the song "Shape of Things to Come," the brilliant rock vocalist Chris Cornell sang, "There's a crack in the clouds, but only for a moment now, like an eye looking out, in blue skies, finds the roads we will go down."[1] In the next section we'll travel down the roads of the housing bubble to see that the Liftoff was driven by the GSEs, Fannie Mae and Freddie Mac. In the late 1960s, the GSEs were insignificant players in housing finance. By the late 1990s, however, their combined share of the national mortgage market had grown to about 40%—they had become a bit like an 800-pound gorilla thrashing about in the basement of a national housing market no longer capable of containing such a beast.

PART III

THE LIFTOFF PHASE
OF THE BUBBLE

-10-

FANNIE AND FREDDIE

The Federal National Mortgage Association (Fannie Mae) was created by the Roosevelt administration in 1938 to provide a source of government support for the home mortgage market. For many years, Fannie remained a relatively obscure agency tucked within the vast alphabet soup of government programs at the Federal Housing Administration, which itself was created during the wave of New Deal legislation in 1934.

Thirty years after its formation, Fannie was still of minimal importance. Out of $412 billion of total mortgage debt in 1968, only 6% was held by *all* federal and related agencies, including Fannie Mae. Roughly three-quarters of all mortgage debt outstanding in the late 1960s was owned by financial institutions such as banks, savings and loans, and insurance companies. (The balance was held by individuals and miscellaneous other investors.)

As evidenced by the post–World War II housing boom, the fact that federal agencies had played a relatively minor role in the mortgage industry did *not* keep the industry from growing substantially in the postwar years. Overall mortgage debt outstanding grew from a little over $70 billion in 1950 to $475 billion twenty years later, representing a compound annual growth rate of about 10% per year.

This rate of growth in the mortgage market was roughly 50% higher than the growth rate of the overall economy.

While the national market for home loans grew rapidly, however, by the late 1960s, severe problems arose in the regulatory structure for the deposit-based institutions (banks and S&Ls) that dominated housing finance. A Congressional Budget Office study from 1996 described one aspect of the problem:

> A prospective home buyer with a steady income, good credit record, and down payment in hand might have been turned down for a loan simply because of a local shortage of funds for lending. Commercial banks, savings and loan associations, and mutual savings banks provided most mortgage finance with funds they had gathered by accepting local savings deposits. Many lenders faced limits on their authority to operate branches outside their home market area and were thus restricted in their ability to make loans and acquire deposits.
>
> Those geographical restrictions tended to isolate local markets for home mortgages from one another. Regions experiencing rapid economic and population growth in the 1960s and 1970s, such as Florida and California, suffered a chronic shortage of loanable funds, whereas other, slower-growing regions, including parts of the upper Midwest and East, often had an excess of funds available for lending.[1]

In essence, the regulatory structure that restricted branch banking kept money from flowing to the housing markets that most needed it, which led to shortages of housing capital in rapidly growing regions of the country. In addition to these geographical issues, the CBO report noted how the availability of housing finance also suffered from regulatory limitations on interest rates under what was known as Regulation Q:

An additional factor periodically hampered lending—namely, the Federal Reserve's Regulation Q, which limited the interest rates that member banks were permitted to pay to attract deposits. When interest rates in the financial markets rose because of inflation or restrictive monetary policy, Regulation Q-type ceilings would prevent depository institutions from matching the rates of interest that savers could obtain on traded securities such as U.S. Treasury bills, notes and bonds. Thus, not only were interregional flows limited, but mortgage markets periodically suffered outflows of funds to the capital markets as savers switched their money from financial intermediaries to direct investment in marketable securities. Through that process of "disintermediation," Regulation Q increased the severity of recessions in regional and national housing markets.[2]

Congress faced a conundrum in trying to deal with these problems. The New Deal's extension of government-guaranteed deposits to banks and S&Ls meant that the government had to regulate these institutions to try to prevent private operators from playing a "heads I win, tails you lose" game with taxpayers' money. At the same time, as the CBO report aptly observed, the New Deal regulatory structure had proved incapable of adapting to meet the needs of an ever-changing economy.

These failures in the regulatory model were not just matters of high finance; they limited the ability of everyday people to buy a home in areas like California and Florida. Given the rising political importance of these areas, it is not surprising that Washington D.C. paid attention. One option for addressing the inefficiencies in housing finance would have been simply to deregulate the industry. This is the approach that the Carter and Reagan administrations later applied to many other areas of the economy, with great success. But the banking regulatory problems arose in the 1960s while Lyndon

Johnson was still working vigorously to expand federal influence through his Great Society programs and Washington still wanted to play a significant role in housing finance.

One problem with the idea of directly expanding the federal government's role, however, was that the combination of LBJ's spending on the Great Society programs and his escalation of the Vietnam War had severely squeezed the federal budget. If Congress tried to solve the problems in housing finance by expanding the role of federal agencies like Fannie Mae, it would have to either raise taxes or increase borrowing—or else the Federal Reserve would have to print even more money to finance these expenditures. None of these options was politically appealing.

Here's how Susan Woodward, a former chief economist for both the Securities and Exchange Commission and the U.S. Department of Housing and Urban Development (HUD), and her co-author Robert Hall described the circumstances: "In the 1960s, there were many pressures on the federal budget, including the war in Viet Nam and the programs of the Great Society, and Fannie Mae's debt, which was at that time counted as part of the federal debt, loomed. A federal budget task force was organized in 1968. One of its assignments was to get Fannie's debt off the federal balance sheet."[3]

Unfortunately, Washington's solution was to turn Fannie Mae into what came to be known as a government-sponsored enterprise (GSE). In 1968, Fannie became a privately owned and funded financial institution. Not wanting to give up its ability to influence housing policy, however, Congress also extended a unique set of privileges to Fannie, including a line of credit with the Treasury Department, an exemption from state and local taxes, and exemptions from having to make certain securities filings that are required of other publicly traded companies.

Private ownership accomplished the objective of moving Fannie's debt off the government's books, but the firm's political privileges led market participants to believe that Fannie's debt carried an implicit government guarantee. Investors believed, correctly, that if Fannie ever failed, the federal government would make good on Fannie's obligations. This was essentially "smoke and mirrors" accounting, an early Washington version of the gamesmanship involving the asset-backed commercial paper conduits that would later help push large private firms like Citigroup to the brink of failure during the financial crisis.

In order to create competition for Fannie Mae, Congress established the Federal Home Loan Mortgage Corporation, commonly called Freddie Mac, as a second GSE in 1970.

The special privileges bestowed upon the GSEs gave them a cost advantage that virtually assured that their influence over housing finance would grow over time. As the CBO report from 1996 put it,

> The agency status of Fannie Mae's and Freddie Mac's obligations transforms the market's view of the credit quality of the housing GSEs and vaults their securities from a rating of A or AA based on their intrinsic financial condition to super AAA because the risk of default is seen to be lower than on even the highest-rated full private securities.[4]

After these reforms, the GSEs enjoyed an enviable position in housing finance. Both the GSEs and the deposit-based institutions (banks and S&Ls) held a fundraising advantage over other private market players. The GSEs benefited from the assumption that they would be bailed out in a crisis, while the banks and S&Ls benefited from the ability to raise government-insured deposits. Hence, both sets of institutions were in an advantageous position relative to private institutions operating without either implicit federal backing or access to federally insured deposits.

In addition to being favorably positioned relative to private operators, the GSEs were also favorably positioned relative to banks and S&Ls, which operated under the regulatory restrictions that kept them from moving savings funds to areas that needed it the most and that limited the interest rates they could pay to attract deposits.

Given these dynamics, Fannie and Freddie began to drive enormous changes in the mortgage market. Previously, banks and S&Ls had long dominated mortgage finance, while federal agencies (including Fannie) played a minor role. Although exact data isn't available, Fannie's share of the mortgage market was below one out of every fifteen single-family loan dollars outstanding in the late 1960s. By the early 1990s, the GSEs' market share had increased to the point where they were involved with about one out of every three dollars of single-family loans.

As the GSEs grew in size and influence, Washington knew that potentially grave dangers lurked. As Warren Buffett, chairman of Berkshire Hathaway, observed in his 2008 shareholder letter: "To aid its oversight, Congress created OFHEO [Office of Housing and Enterprise Oversight] in 1992, admonishing it to make sure the two behemoths were behaving themselves. With that move, Fannie and Freddie became the most intensely-regulated companies of which I am aware, as measured by manpower assigned to the task."

As time would soon tell, even this dedicated regulatory body and the incentives Congress had to oversee the GSEs would prove little match for the enormous political clout amassed by Fannie and Freddie as they drove to exploit the unique privileges that Washington had bestowed upon them. In 1994, Fannie Mae opened its first "partnership offices." Often staffed with Washington insiders, these offices were used to fund and publicize high-profile housing projects in the districts of influential members of Congress. As Bethany McLean observed in a superb exposé that appeared in *Fortune* magazine, "Politicians may not understand the secondary-mortgage market, but they do understand a photo-opportunity and the dispensation of pork."[5]

Then, in 1996, just prior to the upsurge in growth that (as we will soon see) fueled the Liftoff phase of the housing bubble, Fannie dramatically expanded the Fannie Mae Foundation by seeding it with a $350 million gift of its own stock. Buttressed by the rise of Fannie's stock price, the foundation gave Fannie another powerful source of influence peddling. By 2005, Fannie had donated $500 million to numerous organizations affiliated with influential members of Congress. As we will see, this largesse helps explain the escalation of conforming loan limits that helped enable the rapid growth at the GSEs that triggered the Liftoff phase of the bubble.

Again, Mark Twain's famous quote that history doesn't repeat, but it often rhymes, comes to mind. Notice how strikingly similar all of this is to how Andrew Jackson's biographer described Jackson's view that the Second Bank of the United States "made loans to influence elections, paid retainers to pro-Bank lawmakers, and could control much of the nation's economy on a whim."[6]

The special privileges granted to the GSEs were like artificial steroids that enabled their transformation from skinny, 98-pound weaklings on the vast beaches of the national housing market into Mr. Universe bodybuilders. In the late 1960s, the GSEs were involved in less than one out of every fifteen dollars of home loans. By the end of the Liftoff phase of the housing bubble (2001), their market share had risen to nearly one out of every two dollars of home loans outstanding.

Unfortunately, the regulatory model erected to oversee the GSEs did not, in the end, fare much better than the regulatory scheme for depository institutions whose shortcomings had led to the expansion of the GSEs' charter in the first place. In the summer of 2008, Fannie and Freddie both failed. The federal government was finally forced to take the GSEs and their massive debts directly onto the federal balance sheet, thereby undoing decades of financial gimmickry.

−11−

PREVIEW

To understand what caused the housing bubble to lift off in the late 1990s and then accelerate so rapidly during the early 2000s, we need to identify what changed in a housing market that had previously been driven by predominantly regional and local factors and which had functioned so well for so long. Furthermore, the explanation must uncover causes of sufficient magnitude to move a market as enormous as the national housing market, and the consequence of any alleged causes must be sufficient to have threatened the entire U.S. economy with a financial panic the likes of which it had not seen since the Great Depression.

No small order, right?

Nevertheless, both the government-sponsored enterprises and the interest rate policies of the Federal Reserve fit all of these criteria. In this section, I will show that the Liftoff phase of the bubble was caused by the GSEs.

We have already seen that, by the late 1990s, the political privileges bestowed upon the GSEs enabled their market share to grow to the point where, for the first time in history, they had the potential to drive the national housing markets. During the Liftoff, the GSEs' growth rate more than doubled from what it had been during the Base Period. And, just like the sudden spurt that we saw in housing appreciation, the burst of GSE financing occurred suddenly, with growth more than doubling from the last year of the Base Period to the first year of the Liftoff.

Importantly, the GSEs' interest rate margins narrowed during Liftoff. Along with other factors, this tells us that the growth spewing out of the GSEs' was supply-driven. In other words, the increase in housing finance did *not* result from a sudden surge in organic demand coming from homebuyers. This supply-driven conclusion is also consistent with what happened in the rest of the mortgage market where, in sharp contrast to the GSEs, the growth rate actually dropped from the last year of the Base Period to the first year of Liftoff.

The sudden upsurge of GSE growth also pushed the total mortgage market to grow much faster than it had before Liftoff. This is one indicator that the GSEs had grown to the point where they were capable of driving change even in a market as large as housing. I have also prepared pro forma estimates of the impact of the sudden spurt of GSE financings relative to total home sales. These estimates also confirm that the increased financing coming from the GSEs was significant enough to drive national housing appreciation during Liftoff.

Finally, I have analyzed the conforming loan limits that Congress set to help ensure that the GSEs pursued their mission of expanding financing for low- and moderate-income homebuyers. This analysis shows that conforming loan limits also increased rapidly during Liftoff, which shows that the burst of financing suddenly showering down on the housing markets was aided and abetted by federal housing policy.

-12-

THE CAUSE OF THE LIFTOFF

Let's begin by looking more closely at the growth rate of the GSEs.

GSE GROWTH DURING THE LIFTOFF

Table III.1 (following page) shows the total single-family mortgage debt owned or guaranteed by the GSEs—i.e., their total book of business—and the related growth rates from the early 1990s through 2001.

After growing their total book of business at an average annual rate of 7.2% during the Base Period (1994–1997), the GSEs' growth rate more than doubled, to an average rate of 15.1% during the Liftoff. Furthermore, this upsurge in growth happened abruptly. In 1997, the GSEs' book of business grew by just 6.2%. In 1998, the growth rate soared to 16.1%.

Both the sudden surge in GSE financing and the doubling of their average growth rate relative to the Base Period are consistent with the idea that the GSEs triggered the Liftoff phase of the housing bubble.

GSE GROWTH RELATIVE TO THE REST OF THE MORTGAGE MARKET

Of course, it is possible that the sudden and substantial increase in

Mortgage Growth: GSEs

Table III.1

Source of underlying data: Federal Housing Finance Agency, 2014 Report to Congress

Year		GSEs* ($ Millions)	Pct. Chg.	
1994		1,217,952	7.4%	
1995	**Base**	1,301,976	6.9%	
1996	**Period**	1,411,369	8.4%	
1997		1,499,168	6.2%	
Avg. Chg. for Base Period			**7.2%**	
1998		1,740,320	16.1%	*Beginning in '98, GSE mortgage growth spiked upward.*
1999	**Liftoff**	2,008,589	15.4%	
2000	**Phase**	2,212,342	10.1%	
2001		2,629,807	18.9%	*Average growth during Liftoff was over two*
Avg. Chg. for Liftoff			**15.1%**	*times the Base Period growth rate.*

* Represents single-family mortgages owned or guaranteed by Fannie Mae and Freddie Mac

GSE growth was a response to an organic surge in demand for home mortgages. If this had been the case, we would expect to find that growth in the rest of the mortgage market also took off at the same time. Table III.2 expands on the previous table by adding non-GSE single-family mortgages to the presentation.

This table shows that while average annual GSE growth more than doubled from the Base Period to the Liftoff, the average rate of growth in the rest of the single-family mortgage market increased much more modestly, from 5.1% to 6.0%. Further, while GSE growth spiked abruptly—from 6.2% in 1997 to 16.1% in 1998—the growth rate in the rest of the mortgage market actually declined from 6.5% to 4.8% during these years.

These trends are also consistent with the theory that the GSEs caused the onset of the bubble. If the housing markets had lifted off for some reason other than an increase in funds suddenly spewing forth from the GSEs, then non-GSE mortgage debt would almost certainly have spiked upward at a comparable pace. The fact that this did not happen makes it almost certain that the spike in the GSEs' book of business was supply-driven and not demand-driven.

Mortgage Growth: GSEs & Other — Table III.2

Source of underlying data: Federal Housing Finance Agency, 2014 Report to Congress
Federal Housing Finance Agency, Table 4, Single-Family Mortgages Outstanding 1990-2011

Year		Balances ($ Millions)		Pct. Change	
		GSEs*	All Other	GSEs*	All Other
1994		1,217,952	2,059,967	7.4%	4.8%
1995	Base	1,301,976	2,143,407	6.9%	4.1%
1996	Period	1,411,369	2,257,047	8.4%	5.3%
1997		1,499,168	2,403,400	6.2%	6.5%
Avg. Chg. for Base Period				7.2%	5.1%
1998		1,740,320	2,518,697	16.1%	4.8%
1999	Liftoff	2,008,589	2,674,454	15.4%	6.2%
2000	Phase	2,212,342	2,894,238	10.1%	8.2%
2001		2,629,807	3,028,742	18.9%	4.6%
Avg. Chg. for Liftoff				15.1%	6.0%

During Liftoff, the GSEs' growth rate more than doubled, from 7.2% to 15.1%. But the change in growth in the rest of the mortgage market was much more subdued (5.1% to 6.0%). This indicates that the growth spurt at the GSEs was substantially supply-driven.

* Represents single-family mortgages owned or guaranteed by Fannie Mae and Freddie Mac

INTEREST RATE SPREADS

As another test of whether the GSEs' growth was supply-driven, we can look at interest rate spreads. This is simply the difference between what a lender makes on the loans it extends to its customers and the cost that the lender pays to borrow funds to finance these loans. A lender's interest rate spread is much like the difference between the sales price and the cost of goods sold for a manufacturer.

In a mortgage market where *demand* suddenly spikes, we would expect to find that lenders' rate spreads get larger, as lenders respond to the surge in demand by raising their prices (interest rates) relative to their costs. In a market where *supply* surges, we would expect to find just the opposite: that interest rate spreads get smaller as lenders, like the GSEs, effectively lower their prices to help push more money out the door.

Let's take a look at what happened to the GSEs' interest rate spreads over the key phases of the housing bubble.

GSE Interest Rate Spreads   **Table III.3**

Source of underlying data: Value Line

	Fannie Mae			Freddie Mac		
	Avg. Port. Yield	Avg. Int. Pd.	Spread*	Avg. Port. Yield	Avg. Int. Pd.	Spread*
Base Period						
1994	7.80%	6.78%	1.02%	6.31%	5.54%	0.77%
1995	7.56%	6.75%	0.81%	7.15%	5.93%	1.22%
1996	7.70%	6.50%	1.20%	6.94%	5.95%	0.99%
1997	7.65%	6.67%	0.98%	7.77%	6.23%	1.54%
Average Spread – Base Period			**1.00%**			**1.13%**
Liftoff Phase						
1998	7.12%	6.10%	1.02%	6.77%	6.17%	0.60%
1999	6.90%	6.14%	0.76%	6.45%	6.22%	0.23%
2000	7.11%	6.35%	0.76%	6.79%	6.31%	0.48%
2001	7.11%	6.35%	0.76%	6.54%	5.63%	0.91%
Average Spread – Liftoff			**0.83%**			**0.56%**

The drop in average interest rate spread from 1.00% to .83% at Fannie and from 1.13% to .56% at Freddie shows the GSEs effectively lowered pricing during Liftoff, which provides added evidence that their surge in growth was supply-driven.

* Represents Average Portfolio Yield minus Average Interest Rate Paid

Table III.3 shows that Fannie Mae's rate spread during the Base Period was 1.00%. This means that the average yield on its mortgage assets was one percentage point higher than its cost of funds. Freddie's rate spread during the same time was 1.13%.

During the Liftoff phase, however, when both Fannie and Freddie's growth suddenly escalated, their interest rate spreads *narrowed*. In Fannie's case, it decreased from 1.00 to 0.83, which amounts to a 17% drop in what economists would call unit pricing. In Freddie's case, the drop in pricing was more dramatic: its rate spread decreased from 1.13 during the Base Period to 0.56 during Liftoff, a decline of about 50% in unit pricing. The drop in the GSEs' rate spreads during Liftoff provides additional evidence that the sudden burst of growth at the GSEs was supply-driven.

We now know that GSE portfolio growth increased suddenly and dramatically during the Liftoff phase of the housing bubble;

that this growth spurt was unique to the GSEs and not mirrored in the rest of the market; and that rate spreads at the GSEs declined during Liftoff. All of which supports the theory that the GSEs triggered the bubble. Now, let's look at whether the sudden surge in GSE-driven finance was sufficient to move a market as enormous as housing.

WAS GSE GROWTH SUFFICIENT TO MOVE THE MARKETS?

One way to address the question of whether the GSEs were capable of moving the housing markets is to look at the impact of GSE growth on the overall single-family mortgage market.

Table III.4a (following page) shows that the increase in growth at the GSEs, coming at a time when growth in the rest of the mortgage market was relatively subdued, helped push growth in the overall mortgage market up from an annual average of 5.9% during the Base Period to 9.7% during Liftoff.

Now, to demonstrate the impact that the surge in growth at the GSEs had on the increase in overall mortgage financing during the Liftoff, I have prepared an estimate of "excess growth" in mortgages outstanding relative to the Base Period and then calculated how much of it originated from the GSEs. This calculation begins with a pro forma estimate of the amount of mortgage financing that would have existed at the end of the Liftoff phase (1998–2001) if both the GSEs and the rest of the mortgage market had continued to grow at the same rates as they did in the Base Period. Then I subtract this estimate from actual mortgages outstanding to derive an estimate of excess mortgage growth. Finally, I determine what portion of that excess growth came from the GSEs.

The analysis presented in Table III.4b shows that 88% of the excess growth in mortgages outstanding relative to the Base Period originated from the GSEs. This means that GSE growth was the

Mortgage Growth: GSEs, Other, & Total

Table III.4a

Source of underlying data: Federal Housing Finance Agency, 2014 Report to Congress
Federal Housing Finance Agency, Table 4, Single-Family Mortgages Outstanding 1990–2011

Year		Balances ($ Millions)			Pct. Change		
		GSEs*	All Other	Total S.F. Mkt.**	GSEs*	All Other	Total S.F. Mkt.
1994		1,217,952	2,059,967	3,277,919	7.4%	4.8%	5.7%
1995	Base	1,301,976	2,143,407	3,445,383	6.9%	4.1%	5.1%
1996	Period	1,411,369	2,257,047	3,668,416	8.4%	5.3%	6.5%
1997		1,499,168	2,403,400	3,902,568	6.2%	6.5%	6.4%
Avg. Change for Base Period					**7.2%**	**5.1%**	**5.9%**
1998		1,740,320	2,518,697	4,259,017	16.1%	4.8%	9.1%
1999	Liftoff	2,008,589	2,674,454	4,683,043	15.4%	6.2%	10.0%
2000	Phase	2,212,342	2,894,238	5,106,580	10.1%	8.2%	9.0%
2001		2,629,807	3,028,742	5,658,549	18.9%	4.6%	10.8%
Avg. Change for Liftoff					**15.1%**	**6.0%**	**9.7%**

The average growth rate for the total single-family mortgage market jumped from 5.9% prior to the bubble to 9.7% during Liftoff. This shows that the surge in GSE growth was large enough to affect the overall housing markets.

* Represents single-family mortgages owned or guaranteed by Fannie Mae and Freddie Mac
** Represents GSEs plus All Other. S.F. = Single Family

Pro Forma Estimate of Excess Mortgage Growth

Table III.4b

	GSEs – Owned and Guaranteed Mortgages – $ in Millions				All Other Mortgage Providers				Total Excess Growth
	Actual Growth Rate	Actual	Pro Forma	Cumulative Excess	Actual Growth Rate	Actual	Pro Forma	Cumulative Excess	
CAGR	15.1%		7.2%			6.0%	5.1%		
1997		1,499,168	1,499,168			2,403,400	2,403,400		
1998	16.1%	1,740,320	1,607,466	132,854	4.8%	2,518,697	2,527,027	(8,330)	124,524
1999	15.4%	2,008,589	1,723,587	285,002	6.2%	2,674,454	2,657,014	17,440	302,442
2000	10.1%	2,212,342	1,848,097	364,245	8.2%	2,894,238	2,793,686	100,552	464,797
2001	18.9%	2,629,807	1,981,602	648,205	4.6%	3,028,742	2,937,389	91,353	739,558

Summary of Excess Growth

GSEs	648,205	88%
All Other	91,353	12%
Total	739,558	100%

This table shows that excess growth emanating from the GSEs represented 88% of the increase in mortgage financing relative to what would have happened if the GSEs and the rest of the market had continued to grow at the same rates in both the Base and Liftoff periods.

predominant factor behind the sizable increase in the rate of mortgage growth in the entire housing market, which in turn tells us that the spike in GSE financing was capable of affecting the overall housing markets.

Another way to test whether the high growth from the GSEs was sufficient to move the overall housing markets is to estimate the "excess housing investment" (mortgage debt plus equity) spurred by the GSEs during Liftoff, and then compare this estimate to the value of homes sold each year.

As previously noted, real housing prices dropped by an *aggregate* of 1% during the Base Period. This means that home prices essentially grew in line with inflation during this period, which is also consistent with the long-term trend for home price growth. The growth rate of the GSEs during this period therefore provides a reasonable estimate of a rate of mortgage growth that would *not* have triggered the housing bubble.

Table III.5 below takes the pro forma estimates of excess mortgage investment spawned by the GSEs during Liftoff and adjusts for estimated loan-to-value ratios, to arrive at an estimate of excess housing investment (debt plus equity) resulting from the GSEs' rapid expansion.

In the "Actual" column of the table, under "GSEs—Owned and Guaranteed Mortgages," I have set out the actual GSE total book of business for each of the four years of the Liftoff. In the "Pro Forma" column, I show what the GSEs' book of business would have been if their rate of growth had remained the same in 1998–2001 as during the preceding four years.

In the third to last column on the right, I have calculated the estimated excess mortgage debt (over the Base Period trend) generated by the GSEs for each year. In the final column, I have adjusted this excess debt for the effect of down payments, to derive an estimate of total excess investment in housing caused by the GSEs for each year of the housing bubble.

Pro Forma Estimate of GSE-Driven Excess Housing Investment

Table III.5

GSEs – Owned and Guaranteed Mortgages – $ in Millions

	Actual Growth Rate	Actual	Pro Forma	Cumulative Excess	Increase in GSE Owned and Guaranteed			LTV Adjustment*	Estimated Total Excess Inv. in housing
					Actual	Pro Forma	Excess		
CAGR	15.1%		7.2%						
1997		1,499,168	1,499,168						
1998	16.1%	1,740,320	1,607,466	132,854	241,152	108,298	132,854	74%	179,532
1999	15.4%	2,008,589	1,723,587	285,002	268,269	116,121	152,148	75%	202,864
2000	10.1%	2,212,342	1,848,097	364,245	203,753	124,510	79,243	77%	102,913
2001	18.9%	2,629,807	1,981,602	648,205	417,465	133,504	283,961	74%	383,731
					Total Excess	648,205			869,040

The "Actual" column shows actual GSE mortgages outstanding – note the numbers are the same as the first column in Table III.1 presented earlier. The "Pro Forma" column shows what GSE mortgages would have been if their growth rate during Liftoff had been the same as during the Base Period. This enables us to estimate the "Excess" growth resulting from the GSEs' expansion, which in the next table will be compared to total housing sales, which will give a sense of whether the "Excess" growth from the GSEs was significant enough to move housing prices.

* Average Original LTV on new loans from Fannie Mae in 2000 and 2001 annual reports, pages 30 & 32: Note: Freddie only disclosed the distribution of loans at various LTVs without giving an overall average. However, Freddie did disclose original LTV on new purchases which were consistent with the overall averages reported by Fannie and the distribution of loans in the Freddie tables are also consistent with the Fannie LTVs used above.

Now, let's compare this estimate of excess housing investment with the total value of homes sold each year.

The first column of Table III.6 shows the total value of new and existing homes sold during each year of Liftoff. Note that these are actual transaction values, which means they have been affected (pushed up) by the funds flowing out of the GSEs. For this reason, the impact of the estimated excess funds flowing out of the GSEs on the housing markets is somewhat *understated*.

The second column is the estimate of GSE-spawned excess housing investment, as calculated in the final column on the right in Table III.5. The third column in Table III.6 shows the estimated excess investment as a percentage of the value of homes sold each year. The final column shows the real housing appreciation for each year beginning with 1997 and continuing through 2001. The key point in this column is that real housing appreciation was slightly below 1% in 1997, the last year of the Base Period, and then jumped to 4% in 1998, the first year of Liftoff.

As the table shows, the estimated excess housing investment during the Liftoff phase was substantial, averaging about 21% of the actual value of homes sold during this phase.

It's important not to put too fine a point on a pro forma analysis like this. That said, the analysis clearly shows that the estimated excess growth coming from the GSEs was *not* insignificant relative to transaction values. If we had found instead that the estimated excess housing investment represented only a nominal percentage of transaction volume, we would have to question our thesis that the GSEs triggered the housing bubble.

The analysis here demonstrates that the GSEs had amassed so much market share by the late 1990s that the growth spurt they then undertook was capable of moving a market as large as housing, which had previously demonstrated something of an immunity to national influences. To paraphrase the only Nobel Prize–winning rock-and-roller, "the times they had a-changed."[1]

Comparison of Estimated Excess Housing Investment to Actual Sales **Table III.6**

Year	Total Value New and Existing Homes Sold* $ in Millions	Estimated Total Excess Inv. in Housing** $ in Millions	Est. Excess / Value of Homes Sold	Single Family Appreciation (Real)***
1997	799,500			1%
1998	951,254	179,532	19%	4%
1999	1,058,421	202,864	19%	5%
2000	926,598	102,913	11%	5%
2001	1,198,166	383,731	32%	5%
	4,134,439	869,040	21%	5%

This table shows that the estimate of excess housing investment developed in Table III.5 represented 21% of the total value of homes sold during Liftoff. In other words, the "Excess" housing investment spawned by the GSEs was substantial relative to total housing sales. In addition, the far right column shows how the increase in housing investment coincided with the dramatic uptick in home appreciation that began in 1998.

* Source: HUD
** As calculated on Table III.5
*** Underlying data: Robert J. Shiller, Real Home Price Index, See Table II.4

CONFORMING LOAN LIMITS

Before moving on, let's take a moment to discuss the loan limitations the GSEs operated under.

Because Congress originally intended for the benefits of the GSEs' political privileges to flow to low- to moderate-income home-buyers, it set what are called conforming loan limits on the size of GSE loans. Because of the lobbying success of the GSEs and the federal government's belief in increasing homeownership, however, these loan limits were raised significantly over the years. In 1970, the single-family conforming loan limit was $33,000, which is where it remained until it was nearly doubled in 1977. Subsequently the limit was increased in fits and starts, and in 1993, just before the Base Period, it stood at $203,150. Let's take a look at how these loan limits evolved from the Base Period through Liftoff.

GSE Conforming Loan Limits

Table III.7

Source of underlying data: fhfa.gov – data & tools – data – conforming loan limits – history of conforming loan limits

Year		GSE Single-family Conforming Loan Limits	
		1-unit residences	Change
1993		$ 203,150	0.4%
1994		203,150	0.0%
1995	Base Period	203,150	0.0%
1996		207,000	1.9%
1997		214,600	3.7%
Avg. Chg. for Base Period			1.4%
1998		227,150	5.8%
1999	Liftoff Phase	240,000	5.7%
2000		252,700	5.3%
2001		275,000	8.8%
Avg. Chg. for Liftoff			6.4%

The rapid escalation in GSE conforming loan limits — from an average increase of 1.4% before Liftoff to 6.4% during Liftoff — shows that the expansion undertaken by the GSEs was supported by federal housing policy makers.

Conforming loan limits for the GSEs increased by an average of 1.4% per year during the Base Period, and then by 6.4% per year during the Liftoff. This accelerated rate of increase is consistent with the conclusion that the rapid growth in GSE lending was a result of GSE efforts to expand the supply of mortgage financing, *and* it shows that federal housing policy supported this expansion.

According to data from the National Association of Realtors as compiled by HUD, the median price of an existing single-family home in 2001 was $153,100. The GSE conforming loan limit at this time was $275,000, nearly 80% above the median home price, which helps explain how the GSEs had such a large effect on the overall housing markets despite their stated mission to focus on low- to moderate-income homebuyers.

-13-

SUMMARY

The sudden acceleration of GSE growth coincided with the onset of the housing bubble. During the Base Period preceding the bubble, the GSEs' total book of business grew by an average of 7.2% per year. Then, during the four years of Liftoff, their growth rate more than doubled, to an annual average of 15.1%. Just like the spike in housing appreciation rates, the spurt in GSE financing also occurred suddenly and dramatically: their growth more than doubled from the last year of the Base Period to the first year of Liftoff.

The average annual growth rate in the non-GSE portion of the single-family mortgage market increased only modestly, from 5.1% in the Base Period to 6.0% during Liftoff. The absence of a significant acceleration in growth for the non-GSE sector of the mortgage market almost certainly indicates that the sudden expansion in GSE lending was supply-driven, and not the result of a surge in organic demand from homebuyers. The fact that interest rate spreads at the GSEs contracted during the Liftoff is also consistent with this conclusion.

The significant acceleration of GSE growth led to a substantial increase in the growth rate of the overall mortgage market during Liftoff and spawned an increase in housing investment that was significant relative to the volume of home sales. This shows that, by the late 1990s, the substantial market share amassed by the GSEs was sufficient to move the national housing markets.

Finally, the sudden rise in the growth rate of conforming loan limits during the Liftoff shows that the GSE expansion was aided and abetted by federal housing policy.

Based on this analysis, I believe we can safely conclude that the Liftoff phase of the housing bubble was caused by the GSEs, with the support of the federal government. As Credence Clearwater Revival might have put it, beginning in 1998 the GSEs' sudden growth spurt was like a bad moon a-rising over the national housing horizon.

PART IV

THE ACCELERATION PHASE OF THE BUBBLE

-14-

THE MAESTRO

The course of the housing bubble changed dramatically in 2002. After appreciating at the historically remarkable average annual rate of 4.7% during the Liftoff, the average rate of appreciation increased by over 75%, to 8.3%, from 2002 through 2005.

While the GSEs had been the primary drivers of the bubble during the Liftoff phase, things changed during the Acceleration. To be sure, the GSEs were still growing at rates that contributed to the bubble. But the analysis that follows will demonstrate that the Federal Reserve was the primary force behind the escalating rate of housing appreciation in the early 2000s.

The Fed's control over short-term interest rates gave it the potential to affect housing prices on a national basis. Nevertheless, Fed policy had not previously caused anything like what happened during the Acceleration phase. What, then, was different about the early 2000s?

In short, two things had changed. First, the GSEs had sparked a historically unique run-up in housing price appreciation beginning in the late 1990s. Second, the Fed dramatically lowered short-term interest rates in order to deal with the collapse of the Internet stock bubble in 2000 and then held rates at historically low levels through the early 2000s. This pushed interest rates on variable-rate loans below the level of nominal housing price appreciation, thus creating an enormous incentive to buy homes financed with adjustable-rate mortgages rather than long-term fixed-rate mortgages, which had previously dominated home finance. The resulting increase in demand led to the extraordinary acceleration of home price appreciation during the Acceleration phase.

Ironically, Federal Reserve policy during this period was overseen not by a Hamiltonian interventionist, but instead by someone who was viewed as something of a poster child for a more Jeffersonian, free-market approach. Adding further to this confusion, the curmudgeonly man conducting high finance during the Acceleration phase became something of an economic rock star—even as his numerous market interventions belied the free-market reputation that helped him rise to prominence in the first place.

Had we asked John Lennon to unravel this confused intermingling of ideologies and personas, he might have responded with something along the lines of: "I am he as you are he as you are me and we are all together.... I am the walrus, goo goo g'joob!"[1]

In keeping with Lennon's cryptic imagery, let's take a moment to learn a little more about the walrus-masked orchestrator (at one point so admired he was dubbed "the Maestro") whose seemingly self-contradictory policies pushed the housing bubble to such dangerous heights.

Alan Greenspan was the only child of soon-to-be-divorced parents in the Washington Heights neighborhood in the northern part of Manhattan. Like many New York City youngsters growing up in the 1920s and '30s, Alan was far more absorbed with the idea of becoming a big-league ballplayer or a jazz musician than he was with school. "I worked hard at George Washington [High School] but did not get uniformly great grades," he recalled in his autobiography. "When I concentrated I was a good student, and I did really well in math. But I did just okay in courses that didn't interest me because baseball and music took up so much of my time."[2]

Having fallen in love with the jazz great Benny Goodman's music, Alan took up the clarinet in his early teens and, as he put it, "practiced with total dedication, between three and six hours a day." One of his music teachers later gave him the opportunity to play and study with another budding musician in the area, Stan Getz, who would go on to become one of the all-time greats of jazz, often rated in nearly the same class as Miles Davis and John Coltrane. At the time, however, Greenspan's response to playing with the young phenom was a mixture of awe and intimidation: "I knew intuitively that I could never learn to do what he did."[3]

In the mid-1940s, Greenspan enrolled at New York University and took up the study of economics. One of his classmates later described the intellectual environment of the time: "Anyone who was studying economics at that time was determined that there would never be another major depression. The depression of the 1930s had led to World War Two, and so there we were imbued with the sense that we couldn't let this disaster occur again. It was hard to find anyone who was not strongly influenced by the Democratic Party and John Maynard Keynes and his idea about the strong role that government could and should play in dominating economic affairs."[4]

As we saw in the introduction, during the 1940s and '50s, most academics and historians labored under the false belief that the Great Depression had been caused by the underregulated free-market greed of the 1920s. Later, in the early 1960s, the remarkable work of Milton Friedman and Anna Schwartz showed that the Depression in the United States was caused not by private market failure, but rather by the misguided policies of the Federal Reserve.

But we're getting a bit ahead of things here. As a college student back in the mid-1940s, Greenspan found himself uninspired by the heady economic debates of the day. He later explained, "Though...

most of my classmates were ardent Keynesians, I wasn't."[5] Perhaps more interesting, his feelings about all this had little to do with economic philosophy. "I preferred to focus on technical challenges and did not have a macro view. Economic policy didn't interest me."[6]

Greenspan began to take more interest in bigger ideas later on, when his wife introduced him to Ayn Rand: "That's how Ayn Rand and I met. She was a Russian émigré whose novel *The Fountainhead* had been a bestselling phenomenon during the war.... Rand wrote the story to illustrate a philosophy she had come to, one that emphasized reason, individualism, and enlightened self-interest. Later she named it objectivism; today she would be called a libertarian."[7]

Rand was an interesting figure in her own right. As an early exemplar for the feminist movement and the social revolution that would take hold in the 1960s, she had liberal ideas about sexuality, abortion, and race relations. In a pre-feminist world where women were frequently stereotyped as more emotional than men by nature, Rand defied such thinking. As Greenspan observed, "She was a wholly original thinker, sharply analytical, strong-willed, highly principled, and very insistent on rationality as the highest value."[8]

Nevertheless, Rand's staunch belief in free-market capitalism and individualism made her a pariah to an academic and intellectual community that tended to be drawn to communism and other forms of collectivism. Indeed, she is still viewed by many in a distinctly negative light. (By coincidence, I recently looked up another author on Wikipedia, and her profile noted that she had "expressed 'hate' and 'visceral disgust' towards Ayn Rand's book *The Fountainhead*. As she herself indicated, she hates the 'ideas behind it.'")

Whatever her flaws, Rand did not come to her positions lightly. Growing up in Saint Petersburg, Russia, in the early 1900s, she saw firsthand how the Bolshevik Revolution and the Marxist ideology it was based on left a once-thriving culture in a state of impoverished chaos. Even as many Western intellectuals and academics fell for

Marxist ideology and Soviet propaganda, Rand was unwavering in her opposition, refusing to back down from her belief in the preeminence of the individual over the state and in free-market capitalism as the best model for increasing the well-being of *all* members of society.

As time would tell, Rand's economic analysis of communism turned out to be much closer to the mark than that of the Western intellectuals and academics who so despised her. As Greenspan remarked, "The fall of the [Berlin] wall exposed a degree of economic decay so devastating that it astonished even the skeptics. The East German workforce, it turned out, had little more than one-third the productivity of its western counterpart.... The same applied to the population's standard of living.... The extent of the devastation behind the iron curtain had been a very well kept secret, but now the secret was out."[9]

Greenspan also recalled that when the *New York Times* announced the collapse of the Soviet Union, he "felt regret that Ayn Rand hadn't lived to see it. She and Ronald Reagan had been among the few who had predicted decades before that the USSR would ultimately collapse from within."[10]

If Alan Greenspan's identity as a champion of free-market capitalism began to form under the influence of Ayn Rand, his public image as something of a poster boy for these beliefs crystallized when Ronald Reagan appointed him chairman of the Federal Reserve in August 1987. Interestingly, however, the spots on Greenspan's free-market persona soon began to change in ways that few at the time fully appreciated.

-15-

PREVIEW

During the Acceleration phase (2002–2005), the Federal Reserve became the driving force behind the further escalation of real housing price appreciation. By reducing the cost of financing a home to well below the rate of housing appreciation, the Fed spawned a massive increase in demand for short-term variable-rate mortgages on the part of homebuyers wanting to cash in on this historically unusual and seemingly attractive set of circumstances. I say "seemingly" because the apparent opportunity for fast profits created by the combination of the GSE-spawned appreciation and the Fed's interest rates would ultimately lead to enormous losses for millions of people who were drawn by the bubble's glossy allure.

As demand for adjustable-rate mortgages mushroomed, the critical institutions that focused on providing such financing became increasingly exposed to home mortgage assets that they held to facilitate their underwriting business. All of which set up the potential for a financial panic if declining housing prices diminished the value of these assets to the point where the solvency of the critical institutions was threatened.

To borrow again from our Nobel Prize–winning rock-and-roller, the Fed whipped the winds up during the early 2000s even as the markets, policymakers, and regulators—much like everyone over thirty during Dylan's heyday—were generally clueless about the hard rains blowing in from just beyond the horizon. Then again, in defense of both the "older generation" back in the 1960s and most of the participants in the housing bubble of the 2000s, nothing quite like this had ever happened before.

-16-

THE CHANGING ROLE OF THE GSES

By 2001, the GSEs' market share had grown to nearly one out of every two dollars of home loans outstanding, and federal housing policy continued to support their rapid growth. Nevertheless, the GSEs' accounting scandals and the Fed's easy-money policies pushed the GSEs out of the driver's seat of the bubble during the Acceleration phase. Fannie and Freddie continued to grow more rapidly than before the bubble, but their growth during the Acceleration was now more or less in line with the overall market.

CONFORMING LOAN LIMITS

As we have already seen, federal housing policy supported the GSEs' sudden growth spurt that triggered the Liftoff phase (1998–2001) of the bubble. During the preceding Base Period (1994–1997), conforming loan limits grew at an average annual rate of just 1.4%. Then, during Liftoff, conforming loan limits increased by an average of 6.4% per year. Let's now look at what happened during the Acceleration phase.

Table IV.1 shows that conforming loan limits continued their rapid growth during the Acceleration phase, increasing by an average of 7% per year. This shows that the GSEs continued to operate

GSE Conforming Loan Limits

Table IV.1

Source of underlying data: fhfa.gov – data & tools – data – conforming loan limits – history of conforming loan limits

| Year | | GSE Single-family Conforming Loan Limits | |
		1-unit residences	Change
1993		$ 203,150	0.4%
1994		203,150	0.0%
1995	Base Period	203,150	0.0%
1996		207,000	1.9%
1997		214,600	3.7%
Avg. Chg. for Base Period			1.4%
1998		227,150	5.8%
1999	Liftoff Phase	240,000	5.7%
2000		252,700	5.3%
2001		275,000	8.8%
Avg. Chg. for Liftoff			6.4%
2002		300,700	9.3%
2003	Acceleration Phase	322,700	7.3%
2004		333,700	3.4%
2005		359,650	7.8%
Avg. Chg. for Acceleration			7.0%

During Acceleration, conforming loan limits continued to increase at a rapid pace, which shows that federal policies continued to support GSE growth even as the bubble accelerated.

with the full support of their regulators and of Congress, even as the bubble expanded more dangerously. To put it bluntly, their overseers remained unaware of the increasing risks created by their policies. This is not surprising: in the short term, these policy interventions had juiced economic activity, making the overall economy during the late 1990s and early 2000s temporarily more robust than it would have been without these shortsighted interventions.

Meanwhile, the GSEs' aggressive pursuit of market share soon led to other problems.

ACCOUNTING SCANDALS

Flush with the success of the rapid expansion that began in 1998 and the enhanced political power of the foundation that Fannie

Mae had funded, Franklin Raines, Fannie's CEO, proclaimed at an investor conference in early 1999, "The future is so bright that I am willing to set as a goal that our EPS [earnings per share] will double over the next five years." Unfortunately, events would soon reveal that there was more than rapid market-share expansion fueling the GSEs' stock prices.

Arthur Andersen & Co., the large and prominent accounting firm, had long been the auditor of Freddie Mac's financial reports. Andersen's Houston office also audited Enron, the giant energy-trading firm that collapsed in 2001. When Enron's collapse led to the demise of Andersen too, Freddie was forced to change its outside auditor and ended up selecting PricewaterhouseCoopers (PWC).

Arthur Andersen's failure was a wake-up call for the small circle of giant accounting firms that dominated the business of auditing America's largest public companies. Additionally, a number of analysts in the securities industry began to question whether the remarkable predictability and steady growth in earnings then being reported by the GSEs was perhaps a little too good to be true. As Bethany McLean reported in *Fortune*, "John Barnett, then an analyst at the Center for Financial Research and Analysis, which produces detailed reports for institutional investors, suggested that Fannie Mae was distorting economic reality by putting billions of dollars in derivative losses on its balance sheet instead of its income statement."[1]

In this environment of increased vulnerability for the major accounting firms and skepticism over the inordinate predictability of GSE earnings growth, PWC scrutinized its new client's books and came to the conclusion that Freddie Mac had in fact been understating actual earnings in order to smooth out the publicly reported results helping to drive its stock price.

In June 2003, Freddie fired its president and two other senior officials, and federal prosecutors began a criminal investigation into the company's reporting practices. In July, the Office of Housing and Enterprise Oversight (OFHEO), the specially created regulator charged with overseeing the GSEs, announced that Fannie Mae's accounting practices would also be subjected to a special investigation. In late October, adding to all the uncertainty now swirling around the GSEs, Fannie Mae announced a $1 billion revision to balance sheet data included in its early October earnings release.

In September 2004, OFHEO released a report that accused Fannie of also manipulating its reported earnings. This led to an investigation by the Securities and Exchange Commission that essentially confirmed OFHEO's findings, which then resulted in the ouster of Fannie's once highly regarded CEO, Franklin Raines.

The upheaval at the GSEs, and the public scrutiny that came with it, unfolded during the Acceleration phase of the housing bubble. As a testament to the power that the GSEs had accumulated by this point, they continued to grow quite rapidly in spite of these issues. But the scandal did help remove the GSEs from the leading role they had played during the Liftoff.

GSE GROWTH RELATIVE TO THE REST OF THE MORTGAGE MARKET

During the Liftoff phase (1998–2001), the GSEs were the predominant driver of the overall increase in mortgage growth. The relationship between growth at the GSEs and the rest of the single-family mortgage market changed dramatically during the Acceleration phase, however, as shown in Table IV.2.

The key point to focus on in this table is the relationship between growth at the GSEs and growth in the rest of the single-family mortgage market. During the Liftoff phase (1998–2001), the average annual rate of growth for the GSEs increased by 110% while the rate of growth in the rest of the mortgage market increased by less than 20%. This shows that the GSEs were the predominant force driving the escalation in growth in the overall mortgage market during Liftoff.

Mortgage Growth: GSEs, Other, & Total

Table IV.2

Source of underlying data: Federal Housing Finance Agency, 2014 Report to Congress
Federal Housing Finance Agency, Table 4, Single-Family Mortgages Outstanding 1990–2011

Year		Balances ($ Millions)			Pct. Change		
		GSEs*	All Other	Total S.F. Mkt.**	GSEs*	All Other	Total S.F. Mkt.
1994		1,217,952	2,059,967	3,277,919	7.4%	4.8%	5.7%
1995	Base	1,301,976	2,143,407	3,445,383	6.9%	4.1%	5.1%
1996	Period	1,411,369	2,257,047	3,668,416	8.4%	5.3%	6.5%
1997		1,499,168	2,403,400	3,902,568	6.2%	6.5%	6.4%
Avg. Change for Base Period					7.2%	5.1%	5.9%
1998		1,740,320	2,518,697	4,259,017	16.1%	4.8%	9.1%
1999	Liftoff	2,008,589	2,674,454	4,683,043	15.4%	6.2%	10.0%
2000	Phase	2,212,342	2,894,238	5,106,580	10.1%	8.2%	9.0%
2001		2,629,807	3,028,742	5,658,549	18.9%	4.6%	10.8%
Avg. Change for Liftoff					15.1%	6.0%	9.7%
2002		3,023,875	3,389,372	6,413,247	15.0%	11.9%	13.3%
2003	Acceleration	3,458,448	3,781,621	7,240,069	14.4%	11.6%	12.9%
2004	Phase	3,631,743	4,639,671	8,271,414	5.0%	22.7%	14.2%
2005		3,815,917	5,570,718	9,386,635	5.1%	20.1%	13.5%
Avg. Change for Acceleration					9.9%	16.6%	13.5%

During Liftoff, surging GSE growth predominantly pushed total mortgage growth up from an average of 5.9% during the Base Period to 9.7% during Liftoff.

During the Acceleration, the growth rate of the GSEs subsided while growth from other mortgage providers surged—from an average of 6% during Liftoff to almost 17% during Acceleration. This shows the GSEs did not drive the Acceleration phase of the housing bubble.

* Represents single-family mortgages owned or guaranteed by Fannie Mae and Freddie Mac
** Represents GSEs plus All Other. S.F. = Single Family

As the shaded section in Table IV.2 shows, however, these relationships changed rather dramatically during the Acceleration phase. From 2002 through 2005, the rest of the mortgage market became the driving force behind the acceleration in the housing bubble: the average annual growth in the rest of the mortgage market spiked from 6.0% during Liftoff to 16.6% during the Acceleration, while the rate of growth at the GSEs actually subsided, from an annual average of 15.1% down to 9.9%.

Something important had changed. The GSEs still played a role in pushing the bubble at above historical trends during Acceleration, but the fact that the rest of the market was now growing at a 16.6% clip tells us that the GSEs were no longer the primary force behind the bubble.

INTEREST RATE SPREADS

This changing role of the GSEs is also reflected in their interest rate spreads. During Liftoff, they lowered their pricing relative to their cost of funds, which, along with other factors, showed that their increased mortgage production was supply-driven and *not* a result of rising demand coming organically from the mortgage markets. Let's look at what happened to their interest rate spreads during the Acceleration.

Table IV.3 shows that, unlike what happened during Liftoff, GSE interest rate spreads *expanded* during the Acceleration phase. In other words, pricing became more favorable for the GSEs, which indicates that they were now *responding* to higher demand instead of driving increased demand, as they had previously done.

Had the Beatles been singing, "Baby you can drive my car,"[2] their affections would have had to shift from the GSEs to the Federal Reserve as the bubble transitioned from Liftoff to Acceleration.

GSE Interest Rate Spreads

Table IV.3

Source of underlying data: Value Line

	Fannie Mae			Freddie Mac		
	Avg. Port. Yield	Avg. Int. Pd.	Spread*	Avg. Port. Yield	Avg. Int. Pd.	Spread*
Base Period						
1994	7.80%	6.78%	1.02%	6.31%	5.54%	0.77%
1995	7.56%	6.75%	0.81%	7.15%	5.93%	1.22%
1996	7.70%	6.50%	1.20%	6.94%	5.95%	0.99%
1997	7.65%	6.67%	0.98%	7.77%	6.23%	1.54%
Average Spread – Base Period			*1.00%*			*1.13%*
Liftoff Phase						
1998	7.12%	6.10%	1.02%	6.77%	6.17%	0.60%
1999	6.90%	6.14%	0.76%	6.45%	6.22%	0.23%
2000	7.11%	6.35%	0.76%	6.79%	6.31%	0.48%
2001	7.11%	6.35%	0.76%	6.54%	5.63%	0.91%
Average Spread – Liftoff			*0.83%*			*0.56%*
Acceleration Phase						
2002	7.11%	6.35%	0.76%	5.89%	4.61%	1.28%
2003	6.35%	5.38%	0.97%	4.93%	3.62%	1.31%
2004	4.91%	3.10%	1.81%	4.66%	3.54%	1.12%
2005	5.09%	3.88%	1.21%	4.50%	3.50%	1.00%
Average Spread – Acceleration			*1.19%*			*1.18%*

During Liftoff, the drop in avg. rate spreads at the GSEs helped confirm that their growth during this period was supply-driven.

During Acceleration, the GSEs' rate spreads expanded back to levels consistent with the Base Period before the bubble — this shows that GSE mortgage growth during this period was demand-driven.

* Represents Average Portfolio Yield minus Average Interest Rate Paid

–17–

THE CAUSE OF THE ACCELERATION

As noted earlier, any plausible explanation of the cause of the housing bubble needs to meet a number of critical criteria:

1. It must be historically unique to the period in question.
2. It must coincide with the timing and phases of the bubble.
3. It must have had the potential to affect housing prices throughout the nation.
4. It must have been capable of producing conditions that threatened a financial system with a panic the likes of which had not been seen for over seventy years.

We have now seen that the GSEs met all these requirements with respect to the Liftoff, but also that they were *not* the main drivers of the bubble during the Acceleration phase. The evidence that follows will demonstrate that the Federal Reserve's interest rate policy in the early 2000s met all of these criteria and drove the acceleration of the housing bubble.

First, the Fed's rate policy during this time was historically unique, especially in relation to housing appreciation. In driving the cost of adjustable-rate mortgages (ARMs) below the juiced-up rate of housing appreciation triggered by the GSEs, the Fed unleashed an enormous level of demand for variable-rate financing, which pushed the rate of housing appreciation even higher than during the Liftoff phase.

Second, the timing of the Fed's ultralow rate policy coincided with the more rapid escalation of housing prices during the Acceleration.

Third, the Fed's policy affected interest rates nationally, and the effect, as I will show, was sufficient to move the national housing market.

Finally, as we will see in more detail in Part V, the extraordinary demand for mortgage securities resulting from the Fed's policies pushed mortgage debt up dramatically relative to the size of the economy, thereby leading critical financial institutions to expand their holdings of mortgages, which in turn resulted in systemic exposure to a common asset class (home mortgages) whose values were threatened by declining home prices. This created the potential for a financial panic.

We'll begin with a brief overview of the Fed and its purpose, before examining Fed policy and its consequences during the Acceleration phase of the housing bubble. Then, we'll see how the Fed's interest rate maneuvers in the early 2000s fit into a broader pattern of market interventions dating back to the stock market crash of 1987. When we later discuss the financial panic, we will see how this long period of seemingly successful market interventions created an expectation in the markets that then disintegrated into mass panic when the Fed unexpectedly allowed Lehman Brothers to fail in September 2008.

THE FED IN THEORY AND PRACTICE

The Federal Open Market Committee (FOMC) is a small group of policymakers within the Federal Reserve that meets several times a year to set a target for the federal funds rate, which is the interest rate on overnight loans between banks. While interest rates on these loans are nominally determined by the market, in reality the Fed engages in what are called "open market activities" to push the federal funds rate toward the target established by the FOMC.

Through the open-market purchases of government securities, the Fed either increases the money supply, which lowers interest rates, or reduces the money supply, which raises interest rates. The FOMC operates with a dual mandate: it is supposed to consider both the inflationary consequences of pushing too much money into the system *and* the potential drag on economic output (and therefore on employment) if it contracts the money supply too quickly.

From a more practical standpoint, if the Fed wants to "juice" things a bit, it electronically prints money and injects that money into the system through bond purchases, which lowers the cost of borrowing and spurs economic activity. If the Fed is concerned that inflation might be moving into dangerous territory, it contracts the money supply, which raises interest rates and causes economic activity to diminish.

Or, to expand slightly on a famous analogy offered by the former Fed chairman William McChesney Martin: When the economy is dormant and the Fed senses the need to get the party going, it spikes the economic punchbowl with a shot of "moola." Then, when it begins to worry that the party might be on the verge of spinning out of control, the Fed's job is to remove the punchbowl, thereby saving the economic partygoers from a vicious hangover.

At least that is how it's all supposed to work in theory—and there have been times when the Fed's actions have smoothed out economic outcomes, at least for a while. As noted earlier, during the first fifteen years or so of his tenure as Federal Reserve chairman, Alan Greenspan was dubbed "the Maestro" for his seemingly uncanny ability to assist the remarkable stretch of sustained growth from the early 1980s through the '90s.

At other times, however, the Fed's policy moves have not been so widely admired—in fact, just the opposite. It is now generally accepted by economists of all political stripes that the Fed's misguided policies caused the Great Inflation of the 1970s. Furthermore, it is also widely accepted that misguided Fed policies were a primary cause of the Great Depression of the 1930s. In a speech given in honor of Milton Friedman's ninetieth birthday, the former Fed chair Ben Bernanke stated, "Regarding the Great Depression. You're right, we did it. We're very sorry. But thanks to you we won't do it again."[1]

The Fed's singular ability to exert such an extraordinary and systemic impact on the economy stems from its control of short-term interest rates, which gives it the ability to determine the price of money. In an advanced, credit-driven economy, the Fed has the power to influence everything from auto sales in Alaska to housing prices in Honolulu to stock prices on Wall Street.

In a dynamic and competitive economy like ours, no private institution has the ability to exert anywhere near this type of systemic influence. For example, Walmart was far and away the largest company in America in 2020, with revenues nearly 50% above its nearest rival on the Fortune 500 list. But Walmart's $572 billion of revenue accounted for less than three cents out of every dollar of national economic output.

We have seen how the GSEs had amassed a 40% share of the single-family mortgage market just prior to the Liftoff phase of the housing bubble, which obviously endowed them with the capacity to drive enormous changes in the national housing markets. But even this pales in comparison to the Fed's ability to impact *all sectors* of the economy in *all regions* of the country simultaneously.

So much power emanating from a tiny group of people setting interest rates at the FOMC is a bit reminiscent of when the genie in the Disney film *Aladdin* emerges from his lamp and swells to seemingly universal proportions as his voice booms, "PHENOMENAL COSMIC POWERS"—only to then recede back into the lamp as he squeaks, "itty bitty living space!"

The Fed has an enormous and unmatched ability to influence economic activity, and even though it acts with the good intention of smoothing out economic cycles, on multiple occasions its practices have produced a very different result.

Or, to be a bit more blunt about it, the Fed played a primary causative role in the two worst economic decades of the twentieth century, and as we will see here, the Fed also played a primary role in causing the housing bubble that led to the Financial Crisis of 2008.

FED POLICY DURING THE HOUSING BUBBLE

While Fed policy is influenced by many factors, I believe the best single indicator of whether the Fed is trying to stimulate, restrain, or have a neutral effect on the economy is the *real* federal funds (FF) rate, which is determined by subtracting the current rate of inflation from the current effective FF rate. A low *real* FF rate indicates that the Fed is trying to spike the economic punchbowl, and a high rate means that the Fed is trying to drain the bowl of its stimulating effect.

To get an idea of a rate policy designed to have a neutral effect, let's look at FF rates during a period of years preceding the housing bubble. Over the course of the 1980s and '90s, the real FF rate averaged 3.3%. There was only one year during this two-decade span when the average real FF rate was negative, and that was in 1980, when inflation surged to 13.5% and the effective nominal FF rate was 13.4%. The Fed soon shifted gears in response to this situation by raising the nominal FF rate to 16.4% in 1981.

In fact, the extraordinarily high rates needed in the early '80s to finally choke off the runaway inflation of the '70s (itself caused by the Fed) skews the two-decade average for the real FF rate. This period of draconian rates lasted until 1986, when inflation finally dropped back down to a little under 2%. To eliminate this skewing effect, I have focused on the period after those draconian rates ended. From 1987 through 1999, the real FF rate averaged 2.5%, which provides a good standard for a reasonably neutral policy.

Now, to get a sense of just how deeply the Fed cut interest rates in the early 2000s, let's look at the *nominal* (unadjusted for inflation) FF rate. During the 1987–1999 time span, the nominal FF rate average a little under 6%. At the beginning of 2001, the nominal rate was still about 6%, but then the Fed dramatically lowered it throughout the year in response to the collapse of the Internet stock bubble. By the end of 2001, the Fed had pushed the nominal FF rate down to 1.8%, even as inflation remained relatively normal, averaging 2.8% for the year. As a consequence, the *real* FF rate for the whole of 2001 averaged 1.1%, or *less than half* of the historically neutral *real* rate discussed above.

During the next four years (2002–2005), while the real rate of appreciation in home prices soared to unprecedented heights, the real effective FF rates were: 0.1% in 2002, *minus* 1.1% in 2003, *minus* 1.3% in 2004, and *minus* 0.2% in 2005. Hence, after maintaining the real FF rate at an average of 2.5% from 1987 through 1999, the Fed pushed the rate down to an average of *minus 0.6%* during the Acceleration phase of the housing bubble.

Taylor and Bernanke

One of the earliest and most prominent critics of the Fed's rate policy during the housing bubble was John B. Taylor, a professor of economics at Stanford. In 1992, Taylor proposed what has become known as the "Taylor rule" as a prescription for the Fed's interest rate policy. The rule holds that the Fed, in setting the federal funds rate, should follow a formula based on the relationships between inflation and targeted inflation, and between GDP and potential GDP.

During the long expansion of the 1990s, Fed policy was generally consistent with Taylor's widely respected model.

In a presentation at the 2007 annual meeting of the world's central bankers in Jackson Hole, Wyoming, Taylor showed that actual Fed policy began to deviate from the Taylor rule in late 2001 and that the Fed continued to hold rates well below what the rule prescribed until early 2006.

Taylor set forth a similar analysis in his 2009 book, *Getting Off Track: How Government Actions and Interventions Caused, Prolonged, and Worsened the Financial Crisis*. "I begin by showing that monetary excesses were the main cause of the boom and the resulting bust," he wrote. After documenting the period of Fed easing that lasted from late 2001 until 2006, Taylor then observed: "This deviation of monetary policy from the Taylor rule was unusually large; no greater or more persistent deviation of actual Fed policy had been seen since the turbulent days of the 1970s."[2]

While Taylor's analysis helps show that Fed policy was in fact both stimulative and historically unique during the Acceleration phase, some critics have contested his assertion that it caused the housing bubble, noting that the bubble actually began in the late 1990s but the period of unusually low interest rates didn't begin until 2001. I have addressed this criticism in my analysis, which shows that the bubble had distinct phases. The timing of the Fed's ultralow rates does preclude it from having caused the Liftoff in 1998 but is entirely consistent with the idea that the Fed was the primary driver of the Acceleration phase that began in 2002.

In his 2015 book, *The Courage to Act: A Memoir of a Crisis and Its Aftermath*, former Fed chair Ben Bernanke responded to Taylor's criticisms by posing a hypothetical: "Could monetary policy during the early 2000s have been easy enough to achieve our employment and inflation goals while simultaneously tight enough to significantly moderate the housing boom?" Bernanke then replied to his own question: "It seems highly implausible. Modestly higher interest rates, as implied by Taylor's rule, would have slowed recovery while likely having only small effects on housing prices."[3]

While the Taylor rule is helpful in providing an empirical measure of Fed policy during this time, the inherent opaqueness of multivariable models like Taylor's also opens them up to ultimately irresolvable hypothetical questions like that posed by Bernanke. His response to Taylor somewhat obscures the real issues with respect to the housing bubble, which are rather straightforward:

1. Did the Fed, from 2001 through 2005, attempt to stimulate the economy by substantially lowering interest rates and injecting a shot of liquidity into the system?
2. Did the Fed's low rates play an important role in inflating the housing bubble during the Acceleration phase, which ran from 2002 through 2005?

Let's address each of these questions.

Was Fed policy stimulative?

Again, I believe the real federal funds (FF) rate is the best and most straightforward measure of how easy or restrictive Fed policy is at any point in time. Obviously, there are many potential motivations and considerations that go into selecting the exact FF rate, such as the desire to break runaway inflation in the early 1980s, or to smooth out the impact of the sudden stock market crash in 1987, or to support a Fed-orchestrated "stealth" bailout as with Long-Term Capital Management in 1999 (more on this later), or to seek the perfect rate to balance a range of concerns and potential problems, as Bernanke indicated in his response to Taylor's criticism.

Given the various possibilities, it can be difficult to ascertain the intentions behind a certain rate selection and impossible to know

Real Federal Funds Rate   **Table IV.4**

Sources of underlying data:
Effective FF Rate: Federal Reserve Bank of St. Louis
CPI: Shiller

	Period	Average Real* FF Rate	
Long-Term Avg.	'87–'99	2.5%	*In both the longer-term period and the Base Period prior to the bubble,*
Base Period	'94–'97	2.5%	*the Fed held the real FF rate at about 2.5%...*
Liftoff	'98–'01	2.6%	*...and continued to do so during Liftoff,*
Acceleration	'02–'05	-0.6%	*but then dramatically reduced the FFR during Acceleration.*

* Effective Fed Funds Rate minus C.P.I.

how all of these variables might have been affected by an alternative course of action. But if our goal is simply to determine whether—and to what degree—a chosen rate was designed to stimulate economic activity, then a comparison of the real FF rate to past periods is highly instructive. Table IV.4 summarizes the long-term average real FF rate from 1987 to 1999 and then shows the average for the Base Period, the Liftoff, and the Acceleration.

During the thirteen-year period from 1987 to 1999, the real FF rate averaged 2.5%. In the four-year Base Period (1994–1997) and during the four years of Liftoff (1998–2001), the real FF rate averaged 2.5% and 2.6% respectively. Then, starting in 2002, the Fed held the real FF rate at an average of *minus 0.6%...for four years!*

If the Fed wasn't trying to stimulate the economy with ultralow interest rates in 2002–2005, then what in the world *was* it doing?

Did the Fed's policy affect the housing bubble?

To address the question of whether or not the Fed's stimulative policy had a substantive impact on the housing bubble, let's begin by looking at the circumstantial evidence. Table IV.5 compares the timing of the Fed's interest rate changes with the key phases of the bubble.

Real Federal Funds Rate & Real Home Price Appreciation — Table IV.5

Sources of underlying data:
Effective FF Rate: Federal Reserve Bank of St. Louis
CPI: Shiller

	Period	Average for Period		
		Real* FF Rate	Real Home Price Appreciation	
Base Period	'94–'97	2.5%	-0.2%	The real FF rate and home appreciation were both at normal levels during the Base Period.
Liftoff	'98–'01	2.6%	4.7%	During Liftoff, the real FF was normal; the rise in appreciation was triggered by GSEs, not the Fed.
Acceleration	'02–'05	-0.6%	8.3%	The drop in the FF rate coincided with the spike in home appreciation (from 4.7% to 8.3%) during the Acceleration.
Deceleration	'06	1.7%	3.5%	When the Fed started bringing rates back up to historical norms, the bubble first decelerated ('06), then collapsed ('07).
Collapse – Yr. 1	'07	2.2%	-4.6%	

In the Base Period, the Fed's rate policy was neutral, meaning that the real FF rate was generally consistent with historical norms. During this period, housing appreciation was also consistent with historical norms; real home price increases slightly lagged inflation.

In the Liftoff phase of the bubble, the Fed's rate policy was still neutral, but the expansion at the GSEs drove up real housing prices by an annual average of 4.7% per year.

During the Acceleration phase, the combination of the GSEs' accounting scandals and the Fed's easy money effectively removed the GSEs from the driver's seat of the housing bubble. Nevertheless, real housing appreciation suddenly spiked to an annual average of 8.3%, a pace that was 75% higher than during the Liftoff. This sharp acceleration tells us that, beginning in 2002, something significant changed the course of the bubble.

I will later show that this sudden acceleration of home price appreciation was not the result of an alleged global savings glut, or gradual changes in the regulatory landscape, or changes in

Real Federal Funds Rate & Inflation — Table IV.6

Sources of underlying data:
Effective FF Rate: Federal Reserve Bank of St. Louis
CPI: Shiller

Avg. for Periods		Average for Period		
		Real FF Rate	Inflation	
Base Period	'94–'97	2.5%	2.7%	*Even as the Fed eased monetary policy during Acceleration, inflation remained constant, which shows that the "easy money" did not push up consumer prices.*
Liftoff	'98–'01	2.6%	2.5%	
Acceleration	'02–'05	-0.6%	2.5%	

Real Federal Funds Rate & Real GDP Growth — Table IV.7

Sources of underlying data:
Effective FF Rate: Federal Reserve Bank of St. Louis
CPI: Shiller
GDP: ST. Louis Federal Reserve

Avg. for Periods		Average for Period		
		Real FF Rate	Real GDP Growth	
Base Period	'94–'97	2.5%	3.7%	
Liftoff	'98–'01	2.6%	3.6%	*The Fed's easy money did not drive up real GDP growth.*
Acceleration	'02–'05	-0.6%	3.0%	

building costs or home affordability. There were no developments in any of these areas of sufficient magnitude to have caused such a dramatic and historically unprecedented change in a market as large as housing.

As Table IV.5 (previous page) shows, however, the timing of the Fed's aggressive efforts to stimulate the economy from 2002 through 2005 coincided almost perfectly with the Acceleration phase of the housing bubble.

Furthermore, as Table IV.6 shows, the Fed's stimulus did *not* flow into an upsurge in consumer prices, which remained consistent with prior periods.

Nor did the Fed's stimulus result in a sudden spike in the rate of GDP growth, as Table IV.7 shows.

The Fed's stimulus also did not result in a reemergence of the stock market bubble, as Table IV.8 illustrates.

Real Federal Funds Rate & Stock Prices   Table IV.8

Sources of underlying data:
Effective FF Rate: Federal Reserve Bank of St. Louis
CPI: Shiller
Stock Market Indexes: Economic Report of the President

			Average for Period	
	Avg. for Periods	Real FF Rate	S&P 500 Index	NASDAQ Index
Base Period	'94–'97	2.5%	18.4%	20.1%
Liftoff	'98–'01	2.6%	9.4%	16.7%
Acceleration	'02–'05	-0.6%	1.1%	2.2%

Nor did the Fed's easy money cause an escalation in stock market appreciation.

All of which begs the question: If we know that the Fed engaged in a massive and sustained effort to stimulate the economy starting in 2002 *and* we know that this stimulus did not show up in consumer prices, GDP growth, or the stock market, then where did it go? I believe it is quite clear that the Fed's interest rate policy during this time drove a marked change in the course of the housing bubble, as the rate of real home price appreciation spiked from an annual average of 4.7% during Liftoff to 8.3% from 2002 through 2005.

The Critical Measure

To understand why Fed policy had such a significant impact on the course of the housing bubble, let's return for a moment to the Taylor rule. While the Taylor rule is of value as an empirical measure of how generally tight or loose Fed policy is, I believe there is a better measuring stick for the impact of the Fed's interest rate policy on the housing bubble. The Taylor rule focuses on the relationships between the FF rate, consumer price inflation, and GDP. The critical measure with respect to the housing bubble, however, was the relationship between interest rates and the rate of housing appreciation.

The potential impact of debt financing (leverage) on equity returns is a widely understood concept. However, the importance of the relationship between the cost of debt and the total return from investments financed with debt is less widely understood, even for financially savvy individuals.

In the real world, the application of this concept to housing is complicated by a variety of factors: the tax-favored treatment of mortgage interest; ownership costs such as real estate taxes, insurance and maintenance; and the savings gained from not having to pay rent. Nonetheless, the basic importance of the relationship between the cost of debt and the returns from assets is relatively easy to explain with a few highly simplified examples.

Example 1: Mortgage interest rate exceeds the rate of housing appreciation

Let's begin with a hypothetical case where the interest rate on a mortgage *exceeds* the rate of appreciation on the home it finances, and ignore other complicating variables. Suppose we buy a home for $100,000 with a down payment of $20,000 and an $80,000 mortgage that has a 6% interest rate. For the sake of illustration, let's also assume that the interest on the mortgage does not need to be paid currently, but rather is added to the principal balance of the loan each year. Finally, suppose that the value of the home grows at a nominal rate of 3% annually.

After one year of 3% appreciation, the house is worth $103,000, and after a year of 6% accrued interest the balance on the mortgage is $84,800. Because the cost of the loan is *higher* than the rate of appreciation on the home, the value of our equity in the home has dropped from $20,000 at the time of purchase to $18,200 ($103,000–$84,800) a year later—in other words, we've *lost* $1,800.

Importantly, even though the home itself is appreciating, the value of the equity is declining because the interest rate on the loan exceeds the rate of appreciation on the house. This demonstrates a subtlety of leveraged finance that is easy to overlook: *Leverage enhances equity returns only if the cost of the debt is lower than the return on the asset that the debt helps finance.*

In fact, the relationship between average housing appreciation and the average interest rate on one-year adjustable-rate mortgages (ARMs) in this example is not so far off from the relationship that actually existed during the Base Period prior to the housing bubble (1994–1997). So why did people still buy homes during this period? There are a number of explanations, including financial reasons—in the real world, tax deductibility reduces the cost of the loan, for example—and psychological reasons, such as cultural habits, lifestyle preferences, or the memory of times past when the relationship between interest rates and appreciation was more favorable, to name just a few.

Another reason the example above feels so counterintuitive has to do with the real-world structure of home mortgages, which typically require monthly payments of both interest and principal. Since interest on the loan is paid currently, it doesn't add to the principal balance of the loan and its cost is therefore somewhat hidden from homeowners when they sell their property. Likewise, because monthly loan payments also typically include principal amortization, the balance of the loan is being gradually paid down over time, and such payments are often forgotten at the time of sale.

The key point in this first example is: When the cost of financing a house *exceeds* the rate of home appreciation, the value of equity in the home actually *declines*—even though the home itself is growing in value.

Example 2: Mortgage interest rate equals the rate of housing appreciation

Now, let's change the assumptions in our hypothetical so that the interest rate on the mortgage is *equal to* the rate of appreciation on the home. In this case, we'll assume that the home still appreciates at 3%, but the annual cost of the mortgage is now 3% instead of 6%. We'll also assume that the interest is accrued and added to the principal balance at the time of sale.

In this scenario, because the mortgage rate and the appreciation rate are the same, the value of the equity investment grows at the *same rate* as the appreciation in the home. At the end of one year of 3% appreciation, the home is worth $103,000, but the balance of the mortgage (including accrued interest) with a 3% interest rate is now only $82,400. This leaves an equity value of $20,600—which is exactly a 3% increase from the original $20,000 equity value at the time of purchase.

As these first two examples illustrate, even when an asset financed with debt grows in value, the leverage effect from the debt will not enhance the returns on equity unless the cost of the debt is less than the total return from the asset.

Example 3: Mortgage interest rate is below the rate of housing appreciation

Finally, let's revise our assumptions so that the interest rate on the mortgage is *below* the rate of appreciation on the home. Suppose that the home grows in value at a rate of 6% while the mortgage interest rate is still only 3%. In this case, the value of the home at the end of year one is $106,000 and the payoff on the loan is the same as the previous example, $82,400 (the original balance of $80,000 plus $2,400 of accrued interest). This leaves an equity value of $23,600 ($106,000–$82,400).

In this case, the increased rate of home appreciation is greatly magnified by the leverage—even though the home has appreciated "only" 6%, the equity value has grown by 18%! Obviously, if this were to happen in the real world, it would create a great deal of demand for home purchases from people eager to get in on the game.

In fact, this example is not far from what actually happened when, in the midst of the boom in home prices triggered by the GSEs, the Fed drove down interest rates in the early 2000s and then left them well below the rate of housing appreciation for the next four years. For unsuspecting homebuyers captivated by the twinkling allure of the historically unique circumstances created by the GSEs and the Fed, it must have felt like gazing upon a dream home in the sky... with diamonds, as John Lennon might have put it. Unfortunately, a bit like a '60s rock-and-roller coming down from a drug-induced high, when economic gravity reasserted itself, everything crashed back down to earth.

HISTORICAL INTEREST RATES AND APPRECIATION

Let's now turn to the actual data, beginning with the historical relationship between the interest rate on a one-year adjustable-rate mortgage (ARM) and nominal home appreciation before the housing bubble lifted off. I have focused on one-year ARMs because the rate on these short-term mortgages is heavily influenced by the federal funds rate. The underlying source for historical rates on one-year ARMs is the Federal Reserve Bank of St. Louis, whose data goes back only to 1984, so the longer-term historical period before the Liftoff presented in Table IV.9 is for the fourteen years from 1984 through 1997.

The first column in the table shows the average interest rate on a one-year ARM for the fourteen-year period leading up to the Liftoff and for the four-year Base Period. The second column shows the average *nominal* home price appreciation for these periods, and the third column shows the average rate on a one-year ARM *minus* the average rate of home appreciation.

As the third column shows, the historical relationship between the interest rate on a one-year ARM and nominal home appreciation was roughly like the first hypothetical example discussed earlier. The average short-term interest rate *exceeded* the average nominal rate of home appreciation in both the longer and shorter periods leading up to the bubble. In the fourteen-year period, the interest rate exceeded home appreciation by an average of 3.5% per year, and in the four-year Base Period the difference was 3.2%.

ARM Interest Rates minus Nominal Home Appreciation   Table IV.9

Sources of underlying data: Shiller / Federal Reserve Bank of St. Louis

	Avg / Yr. for period shown			
	Int. Rate 1-Yr. ARM	Nominal Home Apprec.	Int. Rate minus Home Apprec.	During the long and short periods preceding the bubble, interest rates on 1-year ARMs averaged more than 3 percentage points ABOVE the rate of nominal home appreciation.
'84–'97 14-Yr. Avg.*	7.3%	3.9%	3.5%**	
'94–'97 Base Period	5.7%	2.5%	3.2%	

* 1 year ARM data only available back to 1984
** Difference in this line due to rounding

During these periods, home prices basically tracked inflation. *Real* home price appreciation averaged 0.4% per year in the fourteen years ending in 1997 and *minus* 0.2% in the four-year Base Period also ending in 1997.

In normal times, prospective homeowners are likely to make a buy-versus-rent decision based on a number of factors, including cultural and lifestyle preferences as well as the long- and short-term trends in housing appreciation and financing costs. In a more *momentum-oriented* market like the one that began to develop in the late 1990s, however, it is safe to assume that the vast numbers of new buyers attracted into the marketplace tend to be highly sensitive to *recent* trends in housing prices and *current* financing costs. Almost by definition, this is what pulls more speculative buyers into a rising market.

To estimate how prospective buyers were likely thinking about the housing markets as the bubble unfolded, I have calculated a three-year trend of nominal home appreciation for each year beginning with 1998. The trend rate for a given year consists of the appreciation rates for the two prior years plus the current year, divided by three. Table IV.10a shows the results of these calculations.

In 1998, the three-year trend for average *nominal* home appreciation was 3.6%. The supply-driven gusher of funds from the GSEs steadily pushed this trend rate of nominal appreciation up to 7.9% in 2001. This happened just as the Fed aggressively reduced interest

3-Year Trend Rate of Nominal Home Appreciation: Liftoff   **Table IV.10a**

Source of underlying data: Shiller

	Nominal Home Apprec. Trend*	
1998 First Year of Liftoff	3.6%	*During the Liftoff, the growth in mortgage supply*
1999	5.2%	*coming from the GSEs pushed the 3-year trend rate*
2000	7.1%	*of nominal home price appreciation up from 3.6% in*
2001 Final Year of Liftoff	7.9%	*'98 to 7.9% in '01.*

*   Average of nominal appreciation for prior 2 years plus current year.

rates: the nominal FF rate was about 6.0% at the beginning of 2001 and 1.8% at the end of the year.

Now, in the next table, let's add a column for the current-year interest rate on a one-year ARM for each year, and then a third column for the difference between the current rate on the one-year ARM and the trend rate of housing appreciation. Note that a positive rate in the third column means that the interest rate *exceeds* the trend rate of appreciation. Also recall that a positive spread between short-term interest rates and housing appreciation was the historical norm prior to the bubble. For the reasons shown in the examples above, this historically normal condition tends to discourage housing speculation.

Let's focus on the third column in Table IV.10b, which shows the then-current interest rate on a one-year ARM minus the trend rate of home appreciation for the year. As we saw in Table IV.9, the rate on one-year ARMs during the four-year Base Period was about 3.2 percentage points *higher* than the trend rate of home appreciation. In Table IV.10b, we can see that this spread narrowed to 2.0% in 1998, primarily because of the rising trend rate of home appreciation. Then, in 1999 and 2000, the spread between the one-year ARM rate and trend appreciation narrowed further, to the point where it was effectively nil in 2000. Notably, the interest rate on the one-year ARM actually *increased* from 1998 to

ARM Interest Rate minus Trend Home Appreciation: Liftoff — Table IV.10b

Source of underlying data: Shiller, Federal Reserve Bank of St. Louis

	Current Yr. Int. Rate on 1-Yr. ARM	Nominal Home Apprec. Trend*	1-Yr. ARM minus Trend Appr.	
1998 First Year of Liftoff	5.6%	3.6%	2.0%	*ARM interest rates remained*
1999	6.0%	5.2%	0.8%	*ABOVE or roughly equal to trend home appreciation*
2000	7.0%	7.1%	-0.1%	*until...*
2001 Final Year of Liftoff	5.8%	7.9%	-2.1%	*... the last year of Liftoff*

* Average of nominal appreciation for prior 2 years plus current year.

2000, which partially neutralized the quickly rising trend home appreciation rate.

In 2001, the aggressive easing initiated by the Fed helped push the interest rate on a one-year ARM down to 5.8%, which was below the trend appreciation rate (7.9%). This *negative* spread of 2.1 percentage points was due to a modest increase (0.8 percentage points) in the trend appreciation rate in combination with a larger drop (1.2 percentage points) in the interest rate on a one-year ARM, which is to say that declining interest rates accounted for about 60% of the change in the spread.

Next, we'll expand the table to include the years of the Acceleration phase (2002–2005).

Table IV.10c shows that the negative spread between the one-year ARM and trend appreciation widened even further in 2002. In this case, about 80% of the change was due to the decline in the interest rate on the one-year ARM, from 5.8% in 2001 to 4.6% in 2002.

These same dynamics continued in 2003: a sharp increase in the negative spread between the interest rate on a one-year ARM and the trend rate of appreciation was driven primarily by a decrease in interest rates.

In 2004 and 2005, however, the negative spread continued to expand, but during these years the expansion was driven by rapid

ARM Interest Rate minus Trend Home Appreciation: Acceleration Table IV.10c

Source of underlying data: Shiller, Federal Reserve Bank of St. Louis

		Current Yr. Int. Rate on 1-Yr. ARM	Nominal Home Apprec. Trend*	1-Yr. ARM minus Trend Apprec.	
1998		5.6%	3.6%	2.0%	
1999	*Liftoff*	6.0%	5.2%	0.8%	
2000	*Phase*	7.0%	7.1%	-0.1%	
2001		5.8%	7.9%	-2.1%	
2002		4.6%	8.3%	-3.6%	*During Acceleration, the increasingly negative spread between ARM rates and trend appreciation increased the incentive to speculate on home prices.*
2003	*Acceleration*	3.8%	8.5%	-4.7%	
2004	*Phase*	3.9%	10.0%	-6.1%	
2005		4.5%	12.0%	-7.5%	

* Average of nominal appreciation for prior 2 years plus current year.

increases in the trend rate of appreciation, which more than offset an upward trend in ARM interest rates.

In summary: Beginning in 2001 and then continuing through the Acceleration phase, the interest cost of a one-year, adjustable-rate mortgage fell further and further *below* the trend rate of housing appreciation, which created an enormous financial incentive to invest in single-family homes financed with variable-rate mortgages. From 2001 through 2003, the rising spread between home appreciation and ARM interest rates was primarily driven by falling interest rates. In 2004 and 2005, the growing spread owed more to increases in the trend rate of home appreciation, as buyers piled into the seemingly too-good-to-be-true housing market.

Now let's look at how the changing spread between the one-year ARM and trend appreciation compared to the *real* FF rate over the course of the housing bubble.

Although not presented in Table IV.10d, the real FF rate averaged 2.5% for the twelve years ending in 1999 and for the four-year Base Period ending in 1997. As the fourth column in the table shows, the real FF rate was slightly higher in 1998, then dropped back into a fairly normal range in 1999 and 2000.

ARM Interest Rate minus Trend Home Appreciation vs. Real Fed Funds Rate   Table IV.10d

Source of underlying data: Shiller, Federal Reserve Bank of St. Louis

		Current Yr. Int. Rate on 1-Yr. ARM	Nominal Home Apprec. Trend*	1-Yr. ARM minus Trend Apprec.	Current Yr. Effective Real FF Rate**	
1998		5.6%	3.6%	2.0%	3.8%	
1999	**Liftoff**	6.0%	5.2%	0.8%	2.8%	*The far right*
2000	**Phase**	7.0%	7.1%	-0.1%	2.9%	*columns show that*
2001		5.8%	7.9%	-2.1%	1.1%	*the FED's easy money policies*
2002		4.6%	8.3%	-3.6%	0.1%	*coincided with*
2003	**Acceleration**	3.8%	8.5%	-4.7%	-1.1%	*the increasingly negative spread*
2004	**Phase**	3.9%	10.0%	-6.1%	-1.3%	*between ARM rates and trend*
2005		4.5%	12.0%	-7.5%	-0.2%	*appreciation.*

*   Average of nominal appreciation for prior 2 years plus current year.
** FF = Fed Funds

In 2001, however, the easing program initiated by the Fed pushed the real FF rate well below historical norms, which in turn helped push the interest rate on a one-year mortgage down from 7.0% in 2000 to 5.8% in 2001 (see the first column in the table). This helped push the spread between the one-year mortgage and trend appreciation into negative territory, which increased the incentives to invest in homes financed with ARMs.

These dynamics then continued in the next two years (2002–2003), as the real FF rate dropped into negative territory. When the Fed pushed the real FF rate down to historic lows, the interest rate on a one-year ARM declined substantially. In the midst of an already robust trend of housing appreciation, this greatly increased the incentive to buy a home.

MORTGAGE ORIGINATIONS

Let's now look at how these dynamics affected mortgage originations. Table IV.11a develops the average annual single-family mortgage originations for the Base Period, the Liftoff phase, and the Acceleration phase of the bubble.

Growth in Single-Family Mortgage Originations

Table IV.11a

Source of underlying data: FHFA

		Total Avg. Annual Single Family Mortgage Originations ($ Millions)	Pct. Chg. from Prior Period Avg.
'94–'97	Base Period	$764,250	
'98–'01	Liftoff	$1,505,750	97%
'02–'05	Acceleration	$3,217,500	114%

Table IV.11a shows that single-family mortgage originations spiked upward in both the Liftoff and the Acceleration. Originations increased from an annual average of $764 billion during the Base Period ('94–'97) to $1,506 billion in the Liftoff ('98–'01), and then to $3,218 billion in the Acceleration phase ('02–'05). In other words, mortgage originations increased by 97% from Base Period to Liftoff and then by another 114% during Acceleration.

Let's now look more closely at the source of the growth in the Acceleration phase. In the following table, I have broken down total single-family mortgage originations into adjustable-rate mortgages (ARMs) and fixed-rate mortgages (FRMs). As Table IV.11b shows, the Liftoff phase of the bubble was dominated by fixed-rate mortgages (FRMs), originations of which increased by 133% from the Base Period (see the far right column). In contrast, ARM originations during Liftoff increased by only 23%. These figures are consistent with the idea that the GSEs triggered the Liftoff phase of the housing bubble.

In the Acceleration phase, however, ARMs grew much more rapidly. After increasing just 23% during Liftoff, they grew by a remarkable 199% during Acceleration (see the second-to-last column in Table IV.11b). At the same time, the growth rate in FRM originations actually subsided, dropping from 133% during Liftoff to 92% during Acceleration. Both the rapid increase in ARM financing and the drop in the growth of fixed-rate financing are consistent

Growth in ARM & FRM Originations

Table IV.11b

Source of underlying data: FHFA

		Avg. Annual S.F. Mortgage Originations			Pct. Change from Prior Period		
		Total	ARMs*	FRMs*	Total	ARMs*	FRMs*
		($ Millions)					
'94–'97	Base Period	$ 764,250	$ 250,521	$ 513,729			
'98–'01	Liftoff	1,505,750	308,332	1,197,418	97%	23%	133%
'02–'05	Acceleration	3,217,500	922,686	2,294,814	114%	199%	92%

* ARM = Adjustable-Rate Mortgage / FRM = Fixed-Rate Mortgage

Note the 199% spike in ARM mortgages during the Fed's period of easy money.

with the idea that the Fed's rate policy was the main driver of the Acceleration phase.

Now, let's focus on year-by-year changes in ARM originations from Liftoff to Acceleration. Table IV.12 shows just how dramatically ARM originations increased as the Fed pushed short-term rates down.

In 2001, the real FF rate averaged 1.1% (first column in the table), and single-family ARM originations were $368 billion. By 2004, the Fed had pushed the real FF rate down to *minus* 1.3%, and ARM originations had ballooned to $1.1 *trillion* (second column in the table).

In contrast, fixed-rate mortgage (FRM) originations dropped slightly over the same time span, from $1.847 trillion in 2001 to $1.784 trillion in 2004.

I believe the chain of events here is quite clear: The Fed drove down the federal funds rate, which pushed the interest rate on one-year adjustable-rate mortgages below the trend rate of housing appreciation, which greatly increased the incentive to buy homes financed with adjustable-rate mortgages, which in turn became the propellant for the acceleration in the rate of housing appreciation during the early to mid-2000s.

Annual ARM and FRM Originations

Table IV.12

Source of underlying data: FHFA, Federal Reserve Bank of St. Louis

		Effective Real FF Rate**	ARMs*		FRMs*	
			Avg. Annual Originations	Pct. Chg. from Prior Year	Avg. Annual Originations	Pct. Chg. from Prior Year
			($ Millions)		($ Millions)	
1998		3.8%	$ 236,231		$ 1,213,769	
1999	Liftoff	2.8%	317,788	35%	992,211	-18%
2000	Phase	2.9%	311,349	-2%	736,651	-26%
2001		1.1%	367,959	18%	1,847,040	151%
2002		0.1%	613,885	67%	2,271,115	23%
2003	Acceleration	-1.1%	838,691	37%	3,106,309	37%
2004	Phase	-1.3%	1,136,217	35%	1,783,784	-43%
2005		-0.2%	1,101,952	-3%	2,018,047	13%

* ARM = Adjustable-Rate Mortgage
FRM = Fixed-Rate Mortgage
** FF = Federal Funds

From the last year of Liftoff ('01) to '04, ARM originations jumped from $367B to $1,136B even as FRM originations declined modestly. ARMs had become the driving force in the bubble.

Let's now look at two related factors: the magnitude of the sudden spurt in one-year ARMs during the Acceleration phase and the rate spread between one-year ARMs and short-term Treasury securities.

The Magnitude of the Spurt in ARM Financing

If the growth in the overall mortgage market from 2002 through 2005 had dropped back down to more normal levels *and* the growth rate in fixed-rate mortgages (FRMs) had dropped in concert with the dramatic rise in ARMs, then it would be possible to interpret what happened during the Acceleration phase as simply a normal shift in the relative market shares of fixed-rate and adjustable-rate mortgages. In fact, before the housing bubble took off, this type of dynamic actually happened, as the following summary of mortgage originations in the 1990s shows.

Table IV.13a shows that average ARM originations in the four years of the Base Period (1994–1997) were 42% higher than in the

Growth in ARM & FRM Originations: Base Period **Table IV.13a**

Source of underlying data: FHFA

		Avg. Annual S.F. Mortgage Originations			Pct. Change from Prior Period		
		Total	ARMs*	FRMs*	Total	ARMs*	FRMs*
		($ Millions)					
'90–'93	Pre-Base Period	$ 733,510	$ 175,896	$ 557,614			
'94–'97	Base Period	764,250	250,521	513,729	4%	42%	-8%

* ARM = Adjustable-Rate Mortgage
FRM = Fixed-Rate Mortgage

Even though average ARM originations grew 42% during the Base Period, this was largely offset by a corresponding 8% drop in FRMs. Hence, the ARM surge was just a shift in market preference, and growth in the overall mortgage market was only 4%. This was very different from what started to happen during Acceleration.

previous four years. At the same time, however, FRM originations declined by 8% during this time, and the overall mortgage market grew by only 4%. During this period, the rapid growth in ARMs simply reflected a shift in the market share of adjustable-rate mortgages relative to fixed-rate mortgages, and did not evidence a significant influx of new demand. This is why housing prices basically tracked inflation during this period.

What happened during the Acceleration phase (2002–2005) was very different, as Table IV.13b illustrates.

This table shows that, during the Acceleration (2002–2005), FRMs continued to grow rapidly—increasing by 92% relative to the Liftoff phase (1998–2001). At the same time, ARMs grew by 199% and the combined growth of FRMs and ARMs pushed the overall mortgage market up by 114%.

This tells us that the spike in ARMs during the Acceleration did not merely represent a displacement of FRM financing, as had been the case in the Base Period. Rather, the spike in ARM financings during Acceleration came in addition to the already robust growth in FRMs, and therefore represented *incremental* funding flowing into an already rapidly rising market.

Growth in ARM and FRM Originations: Acceleration — Table IV.13b

Source of underlying data: FHFA

		Avg. Annual S.F. Mortgage Originations			Pct. Change from Prior Period		
		Total	ARMs*	FRMs*	Total	ARMs*	FRMs*
		($ Millions)					
'90–'93	Pre-Base Period	$ 733,510	$ 175,896	$ 557,614			
'94–'97	Base Period	764,250	250,521	513,729	4%	42%	-8%
'98–'01	Liftoff	1,505,750	308,332	1,197,418	97%	23%	133%
'02–'05	Acceleration	3,217,500	922,686	2,294,814	114%	199%	92%

* ARM = Adjustable-Rate Mortgage
FRM = Fixed-Rate Mortgage

During the Base Period, overall mortgage growth was contained even though ARM growth increased significantly. Because FRM growth remained high even as ARM financings spiked during Acceleration, growth in the overall mortgage market surged to new heights during this period.

The Surge in ARM Financing Relative to National Home Sales

To gain a sense of whether the magnitude of the spike in ARMs was substantial enough to affect national home prices, let's look at an estimate of the excess housing finance that was coming from ARMs relative to overall housing sales during the Acceleration phase. In Part III, I noted that the effort to gauge the impact of the surge in GSE financing on the housing markets necessarily involves estimates and assumptions, and the same applies to the spike in ARMs. While such calculations can start to feel like an exercise in mental gymnastics, they are necessary in order to test whether a theory of influence was of sufficient magnitude to affect the overall market.

During the Liftoff phase, when the GSEs were driving the housing boom, originations of one-year ARMs grew by 23% relative to the Base Period. If ARM originations had continued to grow at this rate during the Acceleration phase, average annual ARM originations in 2002–2005 would have amounted to about $379.5 billion, as shown in Table IV.14a.

Pro Forma ARM Originations   **Table IV.14a**

Source of underlying data: FHFA

	Phase	Description	(Millions)
'98–'01	Liftoff	Actual Annual Average ARM Originations	$ 308,332
	Liftoff	Actual Growth Rate (from Liftoff Phase Avg.)	23%
'02–'05	Acceleration	**Pro Forma Annual Average ARM Originations**	$ 379,483

ARM = Adjustable-Rate Mortgage	*To estimate the potential impact of the surge in ARMs on the overall housing market, I start by creating a pro forma estimate of what ARM originations would have been during Acceleration if they had grown at the same rate as during the previous 4 years (i.e. during Liftoff).*

Estimated Excess ARM Originations   **Table IV.14b**

Source of underlying data: FHFA

	Phase	Description	(Millions)
'98–'01	Liftoff	Actual Annual Average ARM Originations	$ 308,332
	Liftoff	Actual Growth Rate (from Liftoff Phase Avg.)	23%
'02–'05	Acceleration	**Pro Forma Annual Average ARM Originations**	$ 379,483
	Acceleration	Actual Annual Average ARM Originations	922,686
	Acceleration	Estimated Excess Annual ARM Originations	$ 543,203

ARM = Adjustable-Rate Mortgage	*To estimate excess ARM originations during Acceleration I subtracted the pro forma estimate of $379.5 from actual ARM originations of $922.7. This results in estimated excess ARM originations of $543.2.*

Next, in Table IV.14b, we see that actual originations of ARM mortgages during Acceleration averaged $922.7 billion per year. This is about $543 billion more than the pro forma estimate of $379.5 billion per year, which assumed a constant growth rate in ARM originations from Liftoff to Acceleration.

To estimate the total funds flowing into the housing market from the flood of ARM financing—including money coming both from mortgage debt, as just estimated, and from the equity component of home purchases—we need to adjust the estimate of excess ARM financing by an estimated loan-to-value (LTV) ratio for the period. I was unable to find an average LTV either for the market as a whole

Estimated Excess ARM-Driven Housing Investment   **Table IV.14c**

Source of underlying data: FHFA

	Phase	Description	(Millions)
'98–'01	Liftoff	Actual Annual Average ARM Originations	$ 308,332
	Liftoff	Actual Growth Rate (from Liftoff Phase Avg.)	23%
'02–'05	Acceleration	Pro Forma Annual Average ARM Originations	$ 379,483
	Acceleration	Actual Annual Average ARM Originations	922,686
	Acceleration	Estimated Excess Annual ARM Originations	543,203
		Estimated Loan-to-Value Ratio	70%
		Estimated Excess Housing Investment due to ARMs	$ 776,004

ARM = Adjustable-Rate Mortgage   *To estimate the potential impact of estimated excess ARM originations on the housing market, I then divide by the estimated loan-to-value ratio of .70, which results in an estimated excess housing investment of $776.0.*

or for one-year ARMs. The one identifiable source for LTV ratios during this period that I did find was Fannie Mae's 2005 10-K filing, which reported an annual average LTV of 70% for 2002–2005. I have used this as the estimate for average ARM LTVs.

If we divide the estimated excess annual ARM financing of $543 billion per year by the 70% average LTV, we derive an estimate of $776 billion in excess funds flowing annually into the housing markets because of the influx of ARM financing that followed the Fed's efforts to stimulate the economy in 2001–2005, which is shown in Table IV.14c above.

The total value of new and used homes sold during the Acceleration phase was $7,277 billion, which works out to an average of $1,819 billion per year.

If we divide the estimated $776 billion in average annual excess funds flowing into the housing market by the $1,819 billion in actual average home sales, we find that the estimated excess funds resulting from the flood of ARM financings were over 40% of home sales for each year, as shown in Table IV.14d.

As I've noted previously, even though estimates like this are essential to testing the plausibility of a thesis, it's important not to

Estimated Excess ARM-Driven Housing Investment vs. Actual Sales   **Table IV.14d**

Source of underlying data: FHFA

	Phase	Description	(Millions)
'98–'01	Liftoff	Actual Annual Average ARM Originations	$ 308,332
	Liftoff	Actual Growth Rate (from Liftoff Phase Avg.)	23%
'02–'05	Acceleration	**Pro Forma Annual Average ARM Originations**	$ 379,483
	Acceleration	Actual Annual Average ARM Originations	922,686
	Acceleration	Estimated Excess Annual ARM Originations	543,203
		Estimated Loan-to-Value Ratio	70%
		Estimated Excess Housing Investment due to ARMs	(1) $ 776,004
	Acceleration	Actual Average Annual Home Sales*	(2) 1,819,282
		Est. Excess Housing Investment / Actual (1) / (2)	43%

ARM = Adjustable-Rate Mortgage
* HUD

The final step is to compare the estimated excess investment of $776.0 per year to the actual home sales per year of $1,819.0, which shows that the impact of the Fed's rate policies was substantial.

put too fine a point on this type of pro forma analysis. The main takeaway here is that the estimated amount of excess funds flowing into ARM mortgages was *not insignificant*. If, for example, we had conducted this test and found that new ARM money was something like 1% of annual transaction volume, then we'd have to question whether this factor could have moved home prices. Given that the actual calculation shows that pro forma new ARM financings were 43% of transaction value, however, this analysis supports the theory that the Fed's rate policy drove the Acceleration phase of the housing bubble.

ARM RATE SPREADS

In discussing the GSEs, I noted that the spread between the average interest rate they earned on their mortgage portfolios and the rate they paid to finance those loans narrowed meaningfully during the Liftoff phase. This represented a lowering of the GSEs' pricing, which is an indication that their massive growth during Liftoff was *supply*-driven. In other words, the growth during Liftoff was driven by the expansionary efforts of the GSEs and not by an organic, market-based increase in demand for mortgage financing, which would have pushed the interest rate spread up.

Let's now take a look at spreads on ARM interest rates over the course of the housing bubble. We'll focus on the spread between the effective national average rate on conforming one-year ARMs and the interest rate on a three-month Treasury bill.

As Table IV.15 shows, the average spread for a one-year ARM relative to the three-month T-bill was 1.44% during the fourteen-year period ending in 1997. In the four-year Base Period (1994–1997), the average spread was just 0.72%, but it widened again to 1.45% during the Liftoff phase. Then, in the Acceleration phase, the spread between the one-year ARM and the T-bill expanded rather dramatically, to 2.41%, which works out to roughly a 66% increase from the spread during Liftoff.

The significant increase in the spread between one-year ARMs and the three-month T-bill supports the conclusion that the growth here was *demand*-driven. ARM lenders responded to surging demand by raising the relative pricing of their loans.

The trend of interest rate spreads is consistent with the thesis that the Fed's substantial easing of short-term interest rates in the midst of a housing boom greatly increased the incentive for new homebuyers to enter the market. Many of these new buyers were trying to take advantage of the favorable relationship between the elevated housing appreciation triggered by the GSEs and low ARM interest rates resulting from the Fed's easy-money policies. The spike in demand caused the relative price of ARM financing to rise, but not by enough to offset the favorable gap that had developed between home appreciation and financing costs that had caused demand to surge in the first place.

ARM Interest Rate Spreads   **Table IV.15**

Source of underlying data: Federal Reserve Bank of St. Louis

		Average Rate Spread: 1-Yr. ARM minus 3-Mo. T-Bill	
'84–'97	Long-term average	1.44%	
'94–'97	Base Period	0.72%	
'98–'01	Liftoff	1.45%	*The average interest rate on a 1-year ARM was 1.45% above the average interest rate on a 3-month Treasury bill during Liftoff.*
'02–'05	Acceleration	2.41%	*This rate spread then expanded to 2.41% even as ARM originations surged during Acceleration. This shows that the surge in ARM financing during Acceleration was demand-driven. In other words, the Fed's low rates led to a surge in speculative home buying, which led to a surge in demand for ARM financing coming from homebuyers.*

The significant increase in the relative cost of a one-year ARM during Acceleration adds further support for the conclusion that the Fed's low interest rates were the primary driver of the escalating rate of housing appreciation from 2002 through 2005.

-18-

SUMMARY

The real federal funds rate averaged 2.5% and 2.6% respectively during the Base Period and the Liftoff phase of the housing bubble. The Fed then pushed the real FF rate down to an average of *minus* 0.6% during the Acceleration phase. The massive stimulus provided by the Fed's easy money in the early to mid-2000s did not show up in elevated levels of consumer price inflation, or in above-normal GDP growth, or in a reinflation of the late-1990s stock market bubble. Where then did the stimulus go? Into housing. The timing of the Fed's highly stimulative monetary policy dovetails with the Acceleration phase of the bubble.

John Taylor of Stanford was correct in his assessment that Fed policy was too loose during the early 2000s. Nevertheless, the key dynamic in understanding the effect of the Fed's interest rate policies on the housing market is not the relationship between the FF rate and either consumer price inflation or GDP, as the Taylor rule suggests. Rather, the critical measure is the relationship between the FF rate and the already rapid housing appreciation previously triggered by the GSEs. Interest rates on one-year adjustable-rate mortgages followed the FF rate down to historically low levels even as housing appreciation escalated. Homes were appreciating at a rate that exceeded the cost of adjustable-rate mortgages, which stimulated demand and caused billions of additional dollars to flood into the housing markets. After increasing just 23% during the Liftoff, ARM originations grew by 199% during Acceleration.

The increased ARM funds flooding the housing markets were significant relative to annual single-family home sales, meaning that the magnitude of this development was sufficient to move national housing prices. Further, even though ARM rates were declining both on an absolute basis and relative to housing appreciation, the spread between ARM interest rates and short-term T-bills actually widened, which also supports the theory that the surge in ARM financing was *demand*-driven. Buyers were responding to the incentives that the Fed, unwittingly and disastrously, had created.

PART V

THE FINANCIAL CRISIS

-19-

AN ACE IN THE HOLE

Alan "Ace" Greenberg didn't exactly grow up on the wrong side of the tracks—his family managed a women's clothing store—but then again, he didn't exactly grow up on tracks that were likely to stop at the rarefied heights of Wall Street either.

Greenberg grew up in Oklahoma City dreaming not of Wall Street riches, but rather of athletic stardom and other things; he once commented that he was really into "sports and girls, and not necessarily in that order." Toting those lofty aspirations, he went off to the University of Oklahoma on a football scholarship only to suffer a career-ending injury. From there he transferred to the University of Missouri, where he more or less majored in "getting out." As a friend of his at the time put it, "if he was up until 2 o'clock, it was because he was playing bridge."[1]

In spite of these rather inauspicious beginnings, Greenberg then headed to Wall Street looking for a job. Unfortunately, the lack of an Ivy League degree wasn't the only obstacle he faced. As another friend noted, "Other than the Jewish firms, Wall Street was an inhospitable place for a Jewish boy."[2]

Fortunately, even then, Wall Street was not solely the province of highly pedigreed, so-called "white-shoe" firms (a reference to the white buck suede shoes favored by WASPY Ivy Leaguers). On the other side of the street—or perhaps more aptly, in the back alley—there were scrappy, brass-knuckled meritocracies like Bear Stearns. Whereas the white-shoe firms tended to trade on their Ivy League ties in highbrow lines of business like advising Fortune 500 companies on mergers and acquisitions, the Bear earned its money the hard way: in the cutthroat world of securities trading. Formed on $500,000 of startup capital in the early 1920s, the firm took a tightfisted approach to business that enabled it to survive the stock market crash of 1929 and the Great Depression of the 1930s without having to lay off a single employee.

In the mid-1940s, after being turned down by five other Wall Street firms, Greenberg finally landed a job at the Bear—as a clerk working for the not-so-princely sum of $32.50 per week. Finally in an environment where no one cared much about where you went to school or what kind of shoes you wore, Greenberg began to prove himself. Within a short time, he transitioned into a trading position in risk arbitrage, and then, at the tender age of twenty-five, he was put in charge of the department.

By his early thirties, not even a severe bout with cancer could hold Greenberg back. A former colleague recalled, "Unless you could read his mind, you wouldn't know if he was going to Mayo [Clinic] or the bridge club."[3]

Greenberg's disciplined approach to trading also caught the eye of Bear's CEO, Cy Lewis, who had Greenberg take on some of the trading responsibilities for his own personal portfolio. When Lewis died in 1978, Greenberg took over as the head of the only firm that had seen enough in him to offer him a job.

Even as he rose to such lofty heights, Greenberg never lost the iconoclastic edge that had brought him to the other side of Wall Street in the first place. In fact, he remained the short-sleeved, cigar-chomping figure who still answered his own phone within two rings, loved to sit on the trading floor, and typically spent his evenings and Saturdays playing bridge. In the words of one observer, "Greenberg's overriding message is to always stay 'humble, humble, humble' and be wary of arrogance and complacency, especially in bull markets. 'Humans tend to get sloppy when making money is easy.' That's the time to 'not confuse luck with brains' and remember that 'this picnic will not last.'"[4]

Furthermore, even after reaching the pinnacle of his profession, Greenberg continued to practice humility and respect for others. One of his memos advised employees what to do if they noticed a colleague failing to return phone calls from customers or others within the firm: "If an associate has committed either of those insults, you have a choice. You can stew and complain to members of your immediate family, or you can call me AT ONCE. You will not be bothering me—on the contrary, you will make my day. Nothing makes me happier than helping (in a very gentle and kind way) a wayward employee relearn good manners."[5]

During the roaring bull market of the mid-1980s, just before Alan Greenspan was appointed chairman of the Federal Reserve, Greenberg told his employees, "Things are too good!!... Let us continue to watch the shop and realize that none of us are really very smart. We are just in the right place at the right time."[6]

While pushing and prodding his colleagues to sustain the Bear's remarkable climb up Wall Street's ladder of respectability, Greenberg also managed to help his colleagues keep everything in perspective. Embroiled in one of the many tough market periods his firm survived, he told his troops, "This is nothing next to Auschwitz, Buchenwald or Vietnam.... This market will not get me down. It is just a minor challenge."[7]

Having watched nearly every contemporary Wall Street firm either go out of business or be acquired by a larger organization during his many years guiding the Bear, Greenberg could scarcely have anticipated that the cherished firm he had devoted so much of his life to would ultimately succumb to the same fate. In fact, six years after the Ace stepped down as chairman (he remained on the board of directors), two hedge funds managed by Bear Stearns that held big positions in home mortgage securities collapsed. Though few realized it at the time, these funds not only sounded the Bear's death knell, they also more or less served as canaries in the coalmine of the impending financial crisis. In early 2008, Bear would be the first of the major investment banks to falter and require a historic bailout from the Federal Reserve to support J.P. Morgan's acquisition of the once proudly independent firm.

Later, after the financial crisis, Greenberg commented, "There is no Wall Street. It's gone. There is no Wall Street. It's just a street like Broadway or Madison Avenue now.... The model of the investment banking firm is gone forever. It will never come back, in my opinion." He further noted that Wall Street "is gone because it's been proven without a question of doubt in the last year that a rumor can put any of these firms at peril."[8]

As much as I admired Mr. Greenberg, his extraordinary accomplishments, and his humble, straight-shooter's approach to business, I believe that he was incorrect in this assessment of the Bear's demise. Whenever a marketplace—like housing or investment banking—that has functioned successfully through a century of trials and tribulations suddenly craters, something other than a flaw in the structure of the market is at work—something historically unique that led to the unprecedented collapse.

As will be documented later, in Part VI, if Bear had managed its mortgage exposure in a more prudent manner—as some of its competitors did—the once mighty firm would not have required a federal bailout to support the acquisition in lieu of bankruptcy that saved it from total humiliation. Nor would it have contributed so tragically to the end of the Wall Street the "Ace" had long known and loved.

-20-

THE ROAD TO FINANCIAL RUIN

As the Beatles might have said, it was a "long and winding road"[1] from the beginning of the housing bubble in 1998 to the financial crisis in 2008. The bubble was triggered in the late 1990s by the aggressive expansion of the GSEs, and then driven to more dangerous heights in the 2000s by the interest rate policies of the Federal Reserve. A nearly decade-long rise in housing prices pushed mortgage debt outstanding up to almost three-quarters of GDP in 2007, which inevitably led to systemic exposure to precariously valued mortgage assets at a number of critical financial institutions from across the regulatory spectrum. This created the potential for a crisis.

A failure of any one of the critical institutions—the GSEs, the major commercial banks or the major investment banks—that were highly exposed to mortgages had the potential to cause losses for the money market mutual funds and other providers of short-term capital on which the critical financial institutions all depended. Such losses would almost certainly have caused capital providers to withdraw funding from other similarly exposed institutions, thereby leading to a financial panic. In the event, this is exactly what eventually transpired when, after a number of high-profile bailouts, Lehman Brothers was unexpectedly allowed to fail in September 2008.

While perhaps not widely recognized, a panic ignited by the failure of an investment bank was, like the housing bubble, an unprecedented event. When Kidder Peabody, Salomon Brothers, Drexel Burnham, and EF Hutton failed at various points in the 1980s and '90s, it was because of isolated and *non*systemic circumstances tied to the inherently high-risk nature of the securities business. In each case, those failures took place in a financial system that *lacked* systemic exposure to an economically significant *and* precariously valued asset class, and therefore none of these failures provoked a panic. For that matter, Wall Street's history included nearly a century of investment banks failing for one reason or another without triggering anything like the panic of 2008. (The Great Depression was characterized primarily by the failure of small commercial banks.)

Again, the reason that Lehman Brothers' failure sparked a panic is that the housing bubble had led to systemic and economically significant exposure to precariously valued mortgages throughout the financial system. This meant that the failure of any one large institution could lead the capital markets to retract from other similarly threatened companies, thereby creating a liquidity crunch that caused the entire system to freeze up.

SYSTEMIC MORTGAGE EXPOSURE

When asked about the secret to his legendary athletic longevity, the great baseball pitcher Satchel Paige, who continued throwing into his late fifties, once replied, "Avoid running at all times." If we had asked our ancestors for the secret to surviving the Great Depression of the 1930s, they would probably have said, "Avoid debt at all times."

After the Great Depression, lingering fears of carrying debt into a severe economic downturn helped keep a lid on home mortgage debt. In the last few years of the 1940s, total single-family home mortgages outstanding averaged less than 15% of GDP.

Home Mortgages as a Percentage of GDP: 1960–1994   Table V.1

Source of underlying data: Federal Reserve Bank of St. Louis

Decade Avgs.	Home Mortgages as % of GDP	
'60–'69	28%	*Stagflation and high interest rates arrested mortgage growth in the '70s.*
'70–'79	28%	
5-Year Avgs.		
'80–'84	31%	*Finally getting inflation and interest rates under control in the early '80s led to renewed economic growth and rising levels of mortgage debt.*
'85–'89	37%	
'90–'94	43%	

The post–World War II economy benefited from a series of unique circumstances, including: pent-up economic energy at home, the rebuilding of Europe abroad, diminished international competition resulting from the destruction of Europe and Japan and the withdrawal of Russia and China from the international marketplace, and the resetting of the global financial system. The resulting prosperity gradually helped restore the confidence needed to move beyond the deep-seated fear of debt instilled by the Depression. By the early 1960s, total home mortgage debt relative to the economy had roughly doubled from where it stood at the end of the 1940s. In the first half of the 1960s, home mortgage debt averaged just below 30% of GDP.

The Fed's Great Inflation in the 1970s, the resulting economic stagnation, and then the extraordinarily high interest rates needed in the early 1980s to tame the runaway inflation all tempered demand for debt-based financing. In the first half of the 1980s, total home mortgages outstanding averaged 31% of GDP, just slightly above the average from two decades earlier. Then, in the early 1990s, a combination of declining interest rates, sustained economic growth, rising home prices, and growing optimism helped push mortgage debt outstanding up to an average of 43% of GDP. These trends are reflected in Table V.1 above.

Home Mortgages as a Percentage of GDP: 1994–1997   Table V.2

Source of underlying data: Federal Reserve Bank of St. Louis

	Home Mortgages as % of GDP
1994	43.4%
1995	43.5%
1996	43.8%
1997	43.8%
'94-'97	43.6%

By the mid-'90s the post-stagflation spurt in borrowing had largely run its course—the ratio of mortgage debt to GDP stopped growing as quickly as it had from '80 to '94.

Nominal home price increases in the early 1990s slightly lagged the level of general inflation. As home appreciation subsided, so did the brief growth spurt of mortgage debt outstanding relative to GDP that had lasted from the mid-1980s through the early 1990s. For the four years of the Base Period (1994–1997) preceding the housing bubble, home mortgages outstanding averaged roughly 44% of GDP, about the same as the average for the first half of the 1990s.

The key takeaway here is that home mortgage debt as a percentage of GDP rose by about 15 percentage points during the thirty-year span from the early 1960s to the early 1990s, an average increase of about 5 percentage points per decade.

Now, let's take a more detailed look at the relationship between home mortgage debt and GDP in the Base Period. Table V.2 shows that the ratio of mortgage debt to GDP generally stabilized in the years prior to the onset of the housing bubble. In 1997, the last year before the bubble began, home mortgage debt was 43.8% of GDP, about the same as the previous year and roughly even with where it had been in 1993 (43.7%, not shown in the table).

Ten years later, however, the effects of the housing bubble had changed things dramatically. In 2007, as the bubble reached its zenith, home mortgage debt was 72% of GDP. Over the preceding ten years, mortgage debt as a share of GDP had increased by nearly

Home Mortgages as a Percentage of GDP: 1997–2006   Table V.3

Source of underlying data: Federal Reserve Bank of St. Louis

		Home Mortgages as % of GDP	Increase from prior reading*	
1997	Last year before bubble	44%		*From 1947 to 1997, mortgage debt as a % of GDP had grown about 6.5 percentage points PER DECADE.*
2001	End of Liftoff Phase	50%	7%	*During Liftoff, this ratio increased by 7 points in just 4 years.*
2005	End of Acceleration Phase	69%	18%	*During Acceleration, the ratio increased by an additional 18 points.*
2006	Deceleration	72%	3%	*In the last year of the bubble, the ratio grew by another 3 points.*
			28%	*Over the nine years of the bubble, the ratio grew by 28 points.*

* Differences due to rounding

thirty percentage points. The largest share of this rapid increase in mortgage debt outstanding occurred during the Acceleration and Deceleration phases of the bubble, as is evident in Table V.3.

The housing bubble led to a number of highly consequential developments in the home mortgage market.

First, the bubble pushed home mortgages outstanding to levels that would have caused our Depression-era ancestors to roll over on their nearly debt-free mattresses.

Second, the bubble pushed the mortgage markets to grow at a breakneck pace that was literally without precedent. Recall that the increase in home mortgage debt relative to GDP during the thirty-year period preceding the bubble averaged about 5 percentage points per decade. The 28-point expansion in this measure during the decade from 1997 to 2007 was over *five times* faster.

Third, as was documented in Part IV, the Fed's policies stimulated an extraordinary level of demand for short-term, adjustable-rate home loans. After growing by just 23% during the four years of

Liftoff, ARM originations shot up by 199% during the Acceleration phase, when the Fed's policies drove the bubble.

In addition to pushing up mortgage debt to levels that threatened the entire economy, the unprecedented demand for adjustable-rate mortgages led to a marked change in the way that home purchases were financed, giving rise to the massive growth in mortgage securitizations that the GSEs had helped pioneer and that major players like Citigroup and the investment banks stepped in to service. This resulted in systemic exposure to mortgages at financial institutions spanning the regulatory spectrum, from the GSEs to large commercial banks to the major investment banks. A precipitous drop in the value of mortgage holdings at any of these institutions had the potential to set off a panic in the money markets.

As the following analysis will show, the declining value of single-family mortgages is the thread that connects all the main events of the financial crisis, from the failure of the Bear Stearns hedge funds in the summer of 2007, to the failure and bailouts of Bear itself and the GSEs in early 2008, to the unexpected failure of Lehman Brothers in late summer, to fears that the remaining critical financial institutions at the heart of the crisis (Citigroup, Merrill Lynch, and Bank of America) might also fail, and finally to the resolution of the crisis in early 2009.

The following analysis will also demonstrate that a financial crisis was avoidable even *with* the housing bubble. The financial markets were stressed but not panicked from the onset of the huge mortgage-driven write-downs that began in the fall of 2007 and extended through the bailouts of Bear Stearns and the GSEs. A full-blown panic did not arise until the authorities, under intense political pressure, allowed Lehman to fail. Once triggered, the key to ending the panic was relieving market fears that any of the remaining critical financial institutions at the heart of the crisis—Citigroup, Merrill Lynch, Bank of America—might become the next "Lehman surprise."

-21-

PREVIEW

In the following pages, I'll show how objective data—the S&P 500 and the TED spread, a measure of volatility in the short-term lending markets—can be used to chart the course of the financial crisis. This analysis reveals four stages, distinguished by differing levels of market stress. These stages are:

Awareness (June–October 2007): Problems at hedge funds that were heavily invested in mortgage securities caused a change in market conditions—the markets began to register an awareness of potential risk during this stage, but did not yet evidence the stresses that would soon emerge.

Stress (November 2007–August 2008): Key developments during this stage included significant mortgage-related write-downs and losses at major financial institutions, the unprecedented bailout of Bear Stearns, and bailouts of the GSEs. The financial markets began to evidence stress as these developments unfolded, but they did not yet panic.

Panic (September 2008–February 2009): The authorities' unexpected decision to let Lehman Brothers fail caused the markets to go into a state of panic during this stage.

Recovery (March 2009–): A bailout for the last of the systemically exposed critical financial institutions was publicly announced in January 2009. Shortly thereafter, the markets entered into a sustained recovery.

This analysis reveals that the overall state of the financial markets was generally healthy and that the core problems were limited to a relatively small number of critical institutions that were linked by systemic mortgage exposure in the minds of the short-term money markets. Some of the broad kitchen-sink-like bailout measures undertaken by the authorities undoubtedly helped, but the key to ending the panic was resolving market fears that centered on the critical institutions. The critical institutions represented companies from across the regulatory spectrum, from the heavily regulated GSEs and Citigroup—which was partially regulated by the Federal Reserve—to the more lightly regulated investment banks. The fact that the markets remained stressed until all of these institutions were bailed out tells us that the failure of any one of them could have sent the markets into a tailspin. The stress tests were released in May 2009, well after the markets had begun to recover. These tests revealed what has already been said above: that the broader markets were essentially sound and that the core issues centered on the critical financial institutions that had already been bailed out by then.

-22-

CHARTING THE FINANCIAL CRISIS

THE S&P 500 AND THE TED SPREAD

The S&P 500 index of large capitalization stocks and the TED spread—which measures conditions in the short-term interbank lending markets—will both be used to track market stress during the financial crisis.

The TED spread is the difference between LIBOR (the London Interbank Offered Rate) and the interest rate on a three-month Treasury bill. LIBOR itself is determined by averaging the self-estimated rate that a select group of large banks report they can borrow at. The greater the difference between LIBOR and the rate on a Treasury bill, the greater the stress in the short-term financing markets.

While both the TED and the S&P 500 provide valuable information about market conditions, and while both tell a similar tale of the crisis, I believe that the S&P is the best overall guideline for charting the crisis for a number of reasons.

First, there is perhaps no better measure of the expected impact of financial and world events on overall economic conditions and expectations than the S&P 500. Whereas the TED is narrowly focused on assessing stress in the short-term lending markets, the S&P provides a broad measure of conditions throughout the financial and economic systems. The TED may often react a bit more quickly in sensing stresses in the markets for short-term loans between financial institutions, but the S&P is a better gauge of whether these stresses are likely to affect the broader markets and the economy as a whole.

Second, the S&P, which is calculated from hundreds of millions of completed third-party transactions, is a more objectively determined index. By contrast, LIBOR is based on the self-determined *estimates* of the interest rates that a relatively small number of large institutions (fewer than twenty) report they can borrow at. In fact, though LIBOR is widely used and followed, a scandal developed around self-serving and misleading LIBOR reporting in the late 2000s, which then led to investigations, charges that LIBOR had been rigged since as early as 1991, and ultimately to regulatory changes.

Finally, a period of significantly shifting interest rates, such as the sharp decline that occurred during the financial crisis, makes changes in the TED more difficult to evaluate. The TED is typically quoted in basis points, with each basis point equaling one one-hundredth of a percentage point. For example, when the TED is 50 basis points and the three-month T-bill is at 5.00%, it means that banks participating in the LIBOR survey estimate that they can borrow at a rate of 5.50%. But paying a 50 basis-point spread when three-month T-bills are at 5.00% is different from paying a 50 basis point premium when underlying rates are at 1.00%. In the first case, the premium is 10% of the underlying rate, whereas in the second case it is 50% of the underlying rate. This is no small matter, given that the rate on the three-month T-bill dropped from around 5.00% to as low as 0.05% over the course of the financial crisis.

In short, the S&P provides a broader gauge of market conditions, is objectively determined, and is more straightforward to evaluate in a wide range of interest rate conditions. I will use the S&P to chart the course of the financial crisis, but will also refer to the TED as an indicator of conditions in the short-term lending markets. With a few relatively minor exceptions, both measures tell a similar tale of the financial crisis.

Using the S&P 500 and the TED spread to measure market stress, I have broken the financial crisis down into the four stages discussed below.

-23-

THE AWARENESS STAGE
(JUNE–OCTOBER 2007)

By June 2007, the first cracks appeared in the mountain of mortgages that developed as the housing bubble pushed single-family mortgage debt up from 44% to 72% of GDP over the preceding decade. On June 7, two hedge funds managed by Bear Stearns suspended investor redemptions because of heavy losses in their mortgage holdings. Later in the month, the *Wall Street Journal* reported that the funds had been close to shutting down in May. Soon afterward, Bear announced that it would provide $3 billion in financial support to the funds, but the problems only deepened in July. In the middle of the month, Bear announced that the hedge funds had lost nearly all of their value, and on July 31 the funds declared bankruptcy.

On August 9, the French bank BNP Paribas announced that it was suspending redemptions in two hedge funds it managed that were also heavily exposed to U.S. mortgage securities.

THE BROAD FINANCIAL MARKETS

The S&P 500 had been in a moderate uptrend from 2004 through the early months of 2007, before the announcement of Bear's hedge fund problems brought this upward trend to an end. Nevertheless, there were no signs of the deep market stresses that would become evident later in the year. The S&P sold off in June and July, but then recovered through the end of October.

In hindsight, it is easy to see the hedge fund problems at Bear and BNP as early warnings of the financial stresses to come. But the pattern of the S&P through the summer of 2007 makes it clear that the broader markets had not yet grasped either the historic nature of the collapsing housing bubble or its implications for the financial system as a whole. Let's look at the trend of the S&P 500 from 2004 through 2006 and in the first five months of 2007, before the problems at the Bear Stearns hedge funds were announced.

As Table V.4 shows, the S&P was up in each of the three years from 2004 through 2006, increasing by an average of 0.8% per month. This upward trend continued through May 2007, with the S&P rising by an average of 1.6% per month during this period. Clearly, there was a prolonged and steady trend of increases in the S&P before the problems at the Bear Stearns hedge funds were announced.

The S&P 500 was at 1,530 at the beginning of June 2007. On June 7, Bear Stearns froze redemptions in its mortgage hedge funds, and on June 20 the *Wall Street Journal* reported on the steep losses at the funds. After rising in every month except February in the earlier part of the year, the S&P dropped by 1.8% in June. The index recovered in early July, but then sold off late in the month, around the time that the Bear hedge funds declared bankruptcy, ending the month down by a little over 3%.

Problems with U.S. mortgage securities at the BNP Paribas hedge funds were announced in August, but the S&P was actually up slightly for the month. The index then rose again in the next two months, closing October at 1,549, slightly *above* where it had been at the beginning of June, before the problems in the Bear hedge funds emerged.

The S&P 500: Pre-Crisis Table V.4

Source of underlying data: Yahoo Finance

Period		# of Months	S&P 500 Pct. Change	Avg. Monthly Change S&P 500	
Pre-Crisis					
Jan '04–Dec '04	Three Years Prior	12	9.0%	0.7%	
Jan '05–Dec '05	Two Years Prior	12	3.0%	0.3%	
Jan '06–Dec '06	Prior Year	12	13.6%	1.1%	
Jan '04–Dec '06	Total 3 Years Prior	36	27.6%	0.8%	*In the 3 years ending in 2006, the S&P rose by an average of 0.8% per month.*
Jan '07–May '07	Pre-Awareness	5	7.9%	1.6%	*The upward trend continued in early 2007...*
Jun '07–Oct '07	Awareness	5	1.2%	0.2%	*...but then mortgage problems at hedge funds in the summer of '07 curtailed the index's upward momentum.*

I believe we can read two key developments in the S&P's trail during this period.

First, the problems at Bear clearly affected the broader financial markets. After a steadily rising trend from the beginning of 2004 through May 2007, the S&P dropped in June and July as the markets became aware of the struggles and then the collapse at the Bear funds.

Second, while the broader markets were clearly affected by the surfacing of Bear's mortgage problems, the fact that the S&P recovered and was up slightly by the end of October tells us that the markets were not yet stressed.

Bear's hedge fund problems ended the upward momentum of the S&P, but the index remained relatively quiescent and did not exhibit the stresses that would soon be evident. I believe the broader financial markets initially saw the hedge fund problems as a relatively contained expression of the emerging problems resulting from the end of the housing bubble, but at this point the markets still had no idea of just how precipitously housing prices would fall, or how severely this unprecedented collapse would affect the mortgage markets and the critically exposed financial institutions.

THE SHORT-TERM LENDING MARKETS

Like the S&P, the TED spread initially showed a moderate reaction to Bear's hedge fund problems in June and July. Unlike the S&P, however, the TED showed clear signs of stress in the aftermath of the BNP Paribas announcement.

From 2004 to 2006, the TED averaged 38 basis points, and it hovered around this level for the first three months of 2007. It then climbed a little in April and May, before popping up to 75 basis points in June, when Bear's problems were announced.

The TED settled somewhat in July, but spiked up to 130 basis points with the announcement of BNP's hedge fund problems in August. The TED then remained at these elevated levels during September and October.

SUMMARY OF THE AWARENESS STAGE

The announcement of problems at the hedge funds managed by Bear Stearns and BNP Paribas during the summer of 2007 put the markets on notice that the collapse of the housing bubble was beginning to weigh on the value of mortgage assets tied to U.S. housing values. The interbank lending markets registered stress a bit more quickly than the broader U.S. financial markets, which is not surprising given that the TED, which measures lending conditions for large interbank transactions, was reacting to problems that had arisen in a giant international bank headquartered in France. The S&P 500 initially wobbled, but then stabilized. As would be expected, the TED entered the stress zone a bit before the S&P 500, but the status of these two indicators would soon be in sync.

-24-

THE STRESS STAGE
(NOVEMBER 2007–AUGUST 2008)

On the announcement of problems at the BNP Paribas hedge funds in August 2007, the TED spread hiked up, but the broader U.S. financial markets remained relatively calm through October. As a post-Beatles Paul McCartney might have put it: stresses were knocking at the door, but the markets had not yet let them in. It would not be long, however, before a more alarming wake-up call brought the markets to a higher level of stress.

THE BROAD FINANCIAL MARKETS

The relative calm of the S&P following the hedge fund problems at Bear Stearns came to an end with a string of dire mortgage-related announcements from a number of the nation's largest financial institutions.

Late 2007

In mid-October 2007, Citigroup, Bank of America, and Wachovia all announced steep profit declines due to mortgage write-downs. Even more alarmingly, toward the end of October, Merrill Lynch announced the largest quarterly loss in the firm's history, which then led to the resignation of its CEO on October 30. Early in November, Citigroup revealed pending write-downs of its subprime mortgage investments by somewhere between $8 billion and $11 billion, which then led to the resignation of its CEO and a capital infusion from the Abu Dhabi Investment Authority. Around the same time as the Citigroup announcement, Morgan Stanley announced an estimated write-down of almost $4 billion. About a month later, the estimate was raised to over $9 billion.

The steady drumbeat of massive mortgage write-downs, historic losses, and jettisoned CEOs served as another indicator that the mortgage exposure caused by the housing bubble was the systemic lava bubbling within the volcano that would later erupt into the Panic stage of the crisis. These announcements ended any hope that the housing downturn would be short-lived and also crushed any hope that the effects of the collapse in housing prices would be contained to a handful of narrowly focused hedge funds.

After closing October 2007 at 1,549, the S&P sold off by 5% over the remainder of the year, ending 2007 at 1,468.

To recap: the broader financial markets, as measured by the S&P 500, had started 2007 with a generally steady pattern of monthly increases, which came to an end during the Awareness stage (June–October) and then turned negative in the first few months of the Stress stage. By late 2007, the broader financial markets had begun to exhibit stress that would soon increase.

Early 2008

In January 2008, the distressed sale of the subprime mortgage giant Countrywide Financial to Bank of America was announced, and two large monoline insurers, Ambac and FGIC, lost their AAA credit ratings due to subprime problems. In February, the giant insurance company AIG announced a $5 billion write-down of subprime-related derivatives; the giant Swiss bank UBS reported an $11 billion loss due to write-downs on its Alt-A mortgage holdings; and the auction-rate securities markets failed. In early March, Thornburg Mortgage—a $36 billion lender that would eventually fail—was unable to meet short-term financing obligations, and an investment fund that focused on mortgage securities and was managed by the highly respected Carlyle Group also failed to meet margin calls.

As these events unfolded, the S&P traded down from its December 2007 reading of 1,468 to a close of 1,293 for the first week of March, an unnerving drop of almost 12% in a little over two months.

Then, a funny thing happened on the way to the crisis: Bear Stearns failed—and the market went *up!*

During the week of March 10, Bear Stearns reported an 88% drop in liquid assets, which precipitated the federal bailout that enabled the distressed sale of Bear to J.P. Morgan the following weekend. Interestingly, the S&P sold off by only a touch, less than 1%, during this week. Then, after closing the week of March 10 at 1,288, the S&P *rose* to 1,322 by the end of March, and held these gains with some oscillations through May 2008, when the index closed at 1,400.

Hence, from the end of the week of March 10 when Bear entered into a distressed sale to J.P. Morgan through the end of May, the S&P actually rose by about 9%. What are we to make of this somewhat incongruous reaction to Bear's failure in the midst of mounting mortgage-related problems throughout the system? I believe there were two important factors at play during the first five months of 2008.

First, there was clearly an elevated level of stress in the broader markets in early 2008, as indicated by the 12% drop in the S&P from the beginning of the year through the first week of March. The underlying source of this stress was the accelerating declines in housing prices and the related pressure on mortgage values that caused the string of announced problems recounted above. Nominal home prices—the key to understanding the pressure on the mortgage exposure of lenders and insurers—had declined about 2% in 2007 and were on the way to a decline of almost 9% in 2008, and the markets were increasingly aware of and stressed by the implications for institutions holding large portfolios of mortgage assets.

Second, I think it is clear in retrospect that the bailout of Bear Stearns nevertheless provided a cautious sense of comfort that the Fed would step in to rescue short-term capital providers (such as money market mutual funds) from the potential consequences of their exposure to the remaining critical financial institutions—which at this point primarily consisted of the GSEs, Lehman Brothers and the other investment banks, and Citigroup and Bank of America.

Summer 2008

On June 9, 2008, Lehman Brothers announced a $2.8 billion loss for the firm's fiscal second quarter. By the end of the month, the S&P had dropped from 1,360 to slightly above 1,280, a decline of a little over 6%. While the bailout of Bear had clearly calmed the markets, the bailout also led to a public and political backlash, and the 6% June swoon in reaction to Lehman's escalating problems showed that deep uncertainties about the politics of bailouts still lingered.

In July, however, the markets found additional reassurance in the idea that the federal authorities would continue to intervene in the case of critical financial institutions. On July 13, the Fed invoked special emergency provisions that enabled it to supply bailout financing to the GSEs. At the end of the month, President Bush signed a bipartisan measure to provide additional funds to backstop Fannie Mae and Freddie Mac.

Once again, mixed signals were emerging from the ongoing beat of events. On one hand, the failure of the GSEs showed that collapsing home values and related mortgage problems were continuing to escalate. On the other hand, the authorities' willingness to extend

The S&P 500: Stress Stage **Table V.5**

Source of underlying data: Yahoo Finance

Period		Avg. Monthly Change S&P 500
Pre-Crisis		
Jan '04–Dec '06	Three Years Prior	0.8%
Jan '07–May '07	Pre-Awareness	1.6%
Financial Crisis		
Jun '07–Oct '07	Awareness	0.2%
Nov '07–Aug '08	Stress	-1.7%

A steady drumbeat of write-downs, losses, and CEO dismissals at major financial firms reversed the upward trend in stocks during the Stress stage.

bailout protections to the GSEs seemed to provide another dose of reassurance that the government would continue to backstop the critical financial institutions.

As markets weighed these mixed messages, they held to an uneasy steadiness. After dropping to 1,280 at the end of June (Lehman's massive second-quarter loss was announced on June 9), the S&P was down only 1% in July and then rose a touch in August to close out the Stress stage of the financial crisis at 1,283.

Over the course of the Stress stage (November 2007 to August, 2008), the S&P dropped by a total of 17%. The table of average monthly changes above depicts the shifting currents in the S&P as the problems caused by the collapsing housing bubble emerged during the Awareness stage and then spread during the Stress stage of the crisis.

As Table V.5 shows, the steady upward beat of the market from 2004 through May 2007 skidded to a halt with the announcement of the hedge fund problems at Bear Stearns in the Awareness stage of the crisis. The realization that these problems would go well beyond a few hedge funds came with the string of dire mortgage-related announcements from many of the nation's largest financial firms beginning in mid-October. These announcements pushed the markets into the Stress stage of the crisis and led to the 17% drop in the S&P from November 2007 to August 2008, an average monthly decline of 1.7%.

THE SHORT-TERM LENDING MARKETS

Like the S&P 500, the TED generally remained at stressed but *not* panicked levels as these events unfolded. After averaging 38 basis points (bps) in the three years ending with 2006 and 45 bps during the first five months of 2007, the TED jumped up to an average of 156 bps in the last five months of 2007.

The TED then settled down to a still-stressed average of 107 bps in January and February of 2008, before jumping back up to around 150 bps in March and April in reaction to the bailout-supported sale of Bear Stearns to J.P. Morgan. Beginning in May, however, the TED resettled itself, averaging 103 bps from May to August 2008.

All in all, from August 2007 through August 2008, the TED averaged 131 basis points, which was well above its historic levels—but decidedly below the stratospheric levels it would soon reach.

SUMMARY OF THE STRESS STAGE

The Stress stage of the crisis, as charted by movements in the S&P 500, lasted from November 2007 through August 2008. The broader financial markets sold off by about 5% during the last two months of 2007 in reaction to the first wave of announced mortgage-related problems at many of the nation's major financial institutions. The parade of escalating problems in early 2008 pushed the markets down an additional 9% in the first two months of the year, but then the authorities' willingness to extend bailout financing to an investment bank (Bear Stearns, in March) and to the GSEs (in July) served to hold the broader markets steady, but nervous, thereafter. The S&P started 2008 at just under 1,470 and ended August at a touch over 1,280, a drop of about 13%.

Like the short-term interbank markets, the equity markets were definitely stressed, but not panicked—a tenuous condition about to undergo a dramatic change. As David Bowie might have sung to the GSEs and the Fed, whose policies created these conditions: Where's your shame, you've left us up to our necks in it, time may change me, but you can't trace time.[1]

-25-

THE PANIC STAGE (SEPTEMBER 2008–FEBRUARY 2009)

When Lehman Brothers was unexpectedly allowed to fail on September 15, the money markets lurched into a state of panic.

Money market fund managers are paid in part to use their judgment to determine whether the additional return from a security, such as Lehman's short-term paper, is worth the added risk of owning that security. Such judgments are based on many factors, including both recent and longer-term expectations of how governmental authorities are likely to interact with the markets. While, from one perspective, the bailouts of Bear Stearns and the GSEs were historically unprecedented and subject to much political backlash, from another perspective, these bailouts fit into a longer pattern of escalating government interventions that dated all the way back to Alan Greenspan's efforts to assuage fears after the stock market crash of 1987.

THE COMMITTEE TO SAVE THE WORLD

The February 1999 cover of *Time* magazine featured a photo of Alan Greenspan, the Federal Reserve chairman, with Robert Rubin, the treasury secretary, and Larry Summers, the deputy treasury secretary, hovering supportively behind Greenspan's pinstriped shoulders.[1] In glowing tones, the article recounted the efforts of Greenspan and his cohorts to intervene in various market crises, including:

- The 1987 stock market crash—when the recently appointed Greenspan flooded the system with cash and the stock markets quickly recovered from a harrowing 20% drop.
- The 1995 bailout of foreign lenders following the flood of capital that poured into Mexico after the passage of the North American Free Trade Agreement.
- The U.S.-led and IMF-orchestrated bailout of lenders threatened by the 1997 Asian contagion resulting from the capital that flooded into many developing markets as global trade ramped up.
- The Fed-engineered stealth bailout of the giant hedge fund Long-Term Capital Management (LTCM) in 1998. The highly leveraged LTCM had loaded up on Russian debt that then defaulted, threatening the firms that had provided financing to LTCM. After first convincing a consortium of Wall Street investment banks to provide the funding needed to keep LTCM from tanking, the Fed then somewhat surreptitiously supported this rescue by lowering interest rates, which had the dual effect of propping up the value of LTCM's debt holdings while at the same time juicing the overall business activity of the Wall Street firms that had done the Fed's bidding.

The *Time* article's author, Joshua Ramo, ably summarized how all of the interventions orchestrated by Greenspan, Rubin, and Summers had helped fuel the long-running economic and stock market booms then under way:

Their biggest shield is an astonishingly robust U.S. economy. Growth at year's end [1998] was north of 5%—double what economists had expected—and unemployment is at a 28-year low. By fighting off one collapse after another—and defending their economic policy from political meddling—the three men have so far protected American growth, making investors deliriously, perhaps delusionally, happy in the process.[2]

The apparent success of all these efforts led *Time* to dub Greenspan and his cohorts "the Committee to Save the World." Lurking just beneath the generally laudatory tone of the article, however, was the concern that what all the interventions had really created was a stock market bubble on which the economy had become dangerously dependent: "And in the U.S., growth is more dependent than ever on the stock market—which has been powered to new highs on the back of Greenspan's interest-rate cuts during the fall." Quoting a Morgan Stanley economist, Stephen Roach, Ramo observed, "'If Greenspan's legacy is a stock-market bubble, he will not be treated kindly by history.'"[3]

Unfortunately, while it took a while for all of this to play out, the escalating consequences of these interventions did, in fact, end badly.

In *When Genius Failed: The Rise and Fall of Long-Term Capital*, Roger Lowenstein succinctly described the market expectations created by the rate cuts that followed the Fed-orchestrated Wall Street bailout of LTCM: "On October 15, [1998] the Fed chief cut rates for a second time—a signal that he would cut and keep cutting until liquidity to the system was restored."[4] The continued easing led the markets to conclude that the Fed was indeed committed not just to curtailing the losses but to revitalizing the bull market that was helping fuel economic growth. From November 1998 through January 1999, the Nasdaq rebounded by a remarkable 40%, but this recovery was not to last.

Having temporarily put the tech stock bull back on its feet, Greenspan and the Fed started raising rates in early 1999. Nevertheless, the underlying enthusiasm for the potential of technology and the Internet, combined with the long-developing belief that the so-called Committee to Save the World would do whatever it took to support asset prices, ultimately led to the blow-off in the stock market bubble: the average reading for the Nasdaq in March 2000 was up by over 195% from its average in October 1998.

Then, in April 2000, the tech stock bubble started to collapse. By October, the monthly average for the index had fallen by over 70%, leaving it well below where it had been when the Fed initially cut rates to support the LTCM bailout. The Fed responded to the collapse of the tech stock bubble with the extraordinary multiyear reductions in the federal funds rate that persisted through the mid-2000s. As documented in Part IV, this is what drove the Acceleration phase of the housing bubble.

To summarize: the long string of often-unprecedented financial market rescues engineered by the Committee to Save the World dated all the way back to the 1987 stock market crash and then extended through the Mexican debt crisis in 1995, the Asian contagion in 1997, the Fed-orchestrated stealth bailout of LTCM in 1998, and included the extraordinary lengths that the Fed went to in the early 2000s to rescue the markets from the collapse of the tech stock bubble. By 2008, the markets had more than twenty years of experience in seeing the Fed (with frequent assists from the Treasury) step in to rescue lenders and even equity investors from one crisis after another.

Furthermore, the historic and unprecedented bailouts of Bear Stearns in March 2008 and the GSEs in July were very much in keeping with this long tradition. But then, in September, the Fed unexpectedly allowed Lehman Brothers to fail. The money market mutual funds and others that had provided short-term financing to Lehman, on the expectation that it too would be bailed out if necessary, were caught off guard, which created a panic driven by the fear that other similarly exposed and critical financial institutions might be allowed to fail as well.

So began the Panic stage of the financial crisis.

LEHMAN BROTHERS' FAILURE

September 15, 2008 is a day that will forever live in financial infamy, to paraphrase FDR. This was the day that Lehman Brothers, contrary to expectations, was allowed to fail.

The Broad Financial Markets' Reaction

After being relatively quiescent in the weeks leading up to Lehman's failure, the S&P went into a tailspin following the investment bank's bankruptcy filing. This downward spiral manifested levels of stress far beyond what was seen during the Stress stage of the crisis.

Returning to the trends in the broad financial markets b*efore* Lehman's failure: the S&P had sold off in the first two months of 2008 as mortgage-related problems spread through the financial sector. The markets then rebounded after the bailout of Bear Stearns in March, obviously on the belief that the authorities would continue to bail out the system much as they had for the prior twenty years. Lehman's June announcement of massive losses caused the markets to wobble again, but the bailouts of Fannie and Freddie in July steadied the S&P during July and August.

The S&P was down by less than 1% in each of the last two weeks of August, and up by about 0.8% in the week prior to Lehman's demise. During the week of September 15, when Lehman failed, the index was actually up by 0.3%, but then it dropped 3.3% the next week, followed by gut-wrenching plunges of 9% and 18% respectively in the two weeks after that.

The S&P 500: Panic Stage   **Table V.6**

Source of underlying data: Yahoo Finance

Period		Avg. Monthly Change S&P 500	
Pre-Crisis			
Jan '04–Dec '06	Total 3 Years Prior	0.8%	
Jan '07–May '07	Pre-Awareness	1.6%	
Financial Crisis			
Jun '07–Oct '07	Awareness	0.2%	
Nov '07–Aug '08	Stress	-1.7%	
Sep '08–Feb '09	Panic	-7.1%	*Lehman's unexpected failure in Sept. '08 pushed the stock market into a state of panic.*

Having started September at about 1,282, the S&P plunged to 896 at the end of November—a drop of 30% in just three months. The index increased a touch in December before sinking to 735 at the end of February. All in all, the S&P fell by a jaw-dropping 43% from the beginning of September 2008 to the end of February 2009.

Table V.6 updates the analysis of monthly changes in the S&P that was presented in the discussion of the Stress stage.

This table shows quite clearly that the markets were shocked and unprepared for Lehman's failure. After dropping by an average of 1.7% per month during the Stress stage, the S&P fell by an average of 7.1% per month during the panic that followed Lehman's demise.

The Short-Term Lending Markets' Reaction

The reaction of the TED spread also shows just how unprepared the markets were for Lehman's failure. From the August 2007 announcement of mortgage problems at the BNP Paribas hedge funds through August 2008, the TED averaged about 130 bps. It actually settled down somewhat following the Bear bailout in March, to an average of just 103 bps from May through August, with readings of 117 and 108 in the last two months of this span.

The TED Spread

Table V.7

Source of underlying data: Federal Reserve Bank of St. Louis

	Period	Average TED Spread	
Pre-Crisis			
Jan '04–Dec '06	3 Years before '07	38	The TED spread, a measure of conditions in short-term lending markets, exhibited a similar pattern to the one noted for stocks.
Jan '07–May '07	Pre-Awareness	45	
Financial Crisis			
June '07–July '07	Awareness	64	Early hedge fund problems caused the TED to rise moderately.
Aug '07–Aug '08	Stress	131	As problems escalated, so did the TED.
Sep '08–Dec '08	Panic	231	**Lehman's failure sent the TED into a panic.**
Jan '09–Apr '09	Post-Panic	101	The bailout of Bank of America, the last of the critical financial institutions, finally brought the TED back to pre-Panic levels.
May '09–Dec '09	Normal	31	The stress tests confirmed that the system as a whole was healthy, i.e. that severe problems were largely limited to the critical institutions—which helped return the TED to normal readings.

In the first two weeks of September, the TED registered readings of 115 and 122 bps, respectively. Then, during the week that Lehman failed, the TED shot up to 241 bps and escalated even further in the final week of September. It spiked to an average of 335 bps in October, then settled back to an average of 210 in November and 180 in December. Table V.7 summarizes the change in the TED as the interbank lending markets traversed the financial crisis.

Both the S&P and the TED demonstrate that the Panic stage of the crisis was precipitated by Lehman's failure. Furthermore, I believe that the sudden and extraordinary levels of market stress exhibited in both of these measures provides convincing evidence that the markets were completely unprepared for the authorities' decision to let Lehman fail.

Could Lehman Brothers Have Been Bailed Out?

Some of the authorities involved in the decision to let Lehman

Brothers fail later asserted that they had little choice, given its financial condition. While I greatly admire the work these people did in the face of tremendous financial and political strains, I don't believe this is the case. These assertions are also inconsistent with many other actions taken in the period leading up to and following the crisis.

Ben Bernanke, the Fed chairman at the time, explained the reasoning in *The Courage to Act: A Memoir of a Crisis and Its Aftermath*. He recounted a critical conversation he had with Tim Geithner, president of the New York branch of the Federal Reserve:

> I asked Tim whether it would work for us to lend to Lehman on the broadest possible collateral to try and keep the firm afloat.
>
> "No," Tim said. "We would only be lending into an unstoppable run." He [Geithner] elaborated that, without a buyer to guarantee Lehman's liabilities and to establish the firm's viability, no Fed loan could save it. Even if we lent against Lehman's most marginal assets, its private sector creditors and counterparties would simply take the opportunity to pull their funds as quickly as possible. Moreover, much of the company's value—certainly the part that initially interested [Ken] Lewis [CEO] and Bank of America—was as a going concern, based on its expertise, relationships, and reputation. In a full-blown run, already well under way, the firm's going concern value would be lost immediately, as customers and specialized employees abandoned ship. We would be left holding Lehman's bad assets, having selectively bailed out the creditors who could exit the most quickly, and the firm would fail anyway. "Our whole strategy was based on finding a buyer," Tim said. It was a question of practicality as much as legality. Without a buyer, and with no authority to inject fresh capital or guarantee Lehman's assets, we had no means of saving the firm.[5]

There are a number of issues with respect to the Fed's ability to bail out Lehman, some addressed in the discussion recounted above, others not. First and foremost, there was the issue of whether the Fed had the necessary authority to provide bailout funds under these circumstances. Although not addressed to the Lehman situation, this issue was already covered in *The Courage to Act* by Mr. Bernanke himself with respect to the broad latitude available to the Fed under existing regulations. As he had observed with respect to the bailout of Bear Stearns earlier in the year, "One of these items in particular—letting nondepository institutions like investment banks participate in auctions of Federal Reserve loans—would require a leap over a particularly high psychological hurdle. We would have to invoke the little-known Section 13(3) of the Federal Reserve Act, which authorized the Reserve Banks to lend to virtually any creditworthy person or entity."[6]

Besides taking the unprecedented step of providing bailout assistance to Bear, the authorities had also decided to provide emergency federal assistance to both Fannie Mae and Freddie Mac. The bailout financing provided to the GSEs was *not* conditioned on an acquisition, which, in the passage above, Mr. Bernanke seems to assert would have been necessary for Lehman to survive. It is also worth noting that the Fed was willing to invoke the unusual and exigent circumstances to provide financing to the GSEs even though they were functionally insolvent (i.e., not creditworthy) at the time, which we know to be the case because the government subsequently had to invest over $180 billion to keep them afloat. Given this assistance, the GSEs ultimately survived the crisis without being acquired and in spite of their marginal creditworthiness at the time assistance was provided.

Mr. Bernanke also asserts that it would not have been possible to lend against the going-concern value of Lehman, which had evaporated in the midst of the panic. But how is this different from what the authorities did with respect to the GSEs and AIG—and, as we will see, with Citigroup and Bank of America /Merrill Lynch? All of these firms were in a situation not unlike Lehman's, and yet all received bailout financing, and all survived without experiencing the dire consequences that Geithner (and Bernanke) claimed would have marked Lehman's fate even if it had been bailed out.

Perhaps most revealingly, Mr. Bernanke also acknowledges other considerations that influenced the Fed's decision: "Meanwhile, as what became known as Lehman weekend approached, popular, political, and media views were hardening against the idea of the Fed and the Treasury taking extraordinary measures to prevent the firm's failure."[7] I believe that these political pressures are in fact the real reason for the decision to let Lehman fail. Anyone who lived through this period will recall the withering political resistance to the idea of providing bailouts to other financial institutions, especially Bear Stearns. The decisions made through this period were understandable, although in hindsight obviously not optimal. When the panicked conditions resulting from Lehman's failure became evident, the political winds shifted and the authorities quickly reversed course to implement the kind of bailouts for other institutions that I believe could have been applied to Lehman.

Not surprisingly, the executives at Lehman, many of whom lost enormous sums when the firm failed, were less than enthusiastic (to put it mildly) about being the exception to the bailout policies enacted during this period. I have no sympathy for their complaints, however. Lehman's executives had the authority and the responsibility to capitalize the firm to withstand a "hundred-year financial flood." They didn't do so. Other executives, like those at Goldman Sachs and Morgan Stanley, did, and they were able to raise enough private capital to survive. I believe that Goldman's and Morgan's ability to raise private capital was a direct result of their carrying significantly higher levels of tangible equity relative to their mortgage exposure, as I will show in Part VI.

Was Lehman treated differently from Bear Stearns, Fannie Mae, Freddie Mac, AIG, Citigroup, Bank of America and Merrill Lynch? Yes.

Was Lehman *entitled* to a government bailout? Definitely not. Lehman's management was at fault for failing to capitalize the firm adequately, and they have no one to blame but themselves.

THE "BAILOUT SINK"

In the wake of Lehman's failure, the authorities reversed course and launched a series of interventions in an effort to stem the panic. In the last half of September, the SEC announced a temporary emergency ban on the short-selling of financial stocks. The Treasury Department announced a temporary money market guarantee program to try and stem the loss of short-term funds from money market funds. (I'll have more to say about the money market mutual fund industry in Part VI.) Also, the Fed approved applications from Morgan Stanley and Goldman Sachs to become bank holding companies, thereby giving the investment banks access to the Fed's discount window.

In late September, Congress turned down the Treasury's request to create a Troubled Asset Relief Program (TARP) to help deal with the crisis. Congress then switched directions and approved TARP in the first week of October. Also in early October, the Fed lowered the target on the federal funds rate to 1.5%, a rate cut that was coordinated with other central banks around the world.

In mid-October, the FDIC—the government insurance fund responsible for protecting commercial bank depositors—announced a Temporary Liquidity Guarantee Program to guarantee new senior debt issued by banks and to extend deposit insurance to accounts used for businesses, governments, and nonprofits. Around the same time, the Treasury announced its Capital Purchase Program, which used TARP funds to make $125 billion of direct investments in a consortium of nine major commercial and investment banks that collectively represented roughly 70% of the nation's financial assets. These investments were funded late in October, around the time that the Fed cut the federal funds rate again, this time to 1.0%.

In late November, the Fed announced that it planned to buy up to $500 million of GSE-issued debt and mortgage securities in order to support the housing markets. Additionally, the Fed again invoked Section 13(3)—which allowed it to lend to virtually any creditworthy entity—and worked with the Treasury to create the Term Asset-Backed Securities Loan Facility, designed to shore up lending in various asset-backed securities markets such as credit cards, student loans, and auto loans. But as Ben Bernanke later acknowledged, "given the complexities involved in setting up the facility, it would not extend its first loan until four months later."[8] (By that time, as we will see, the crisis would effectively be over.)

In mid-December, the Fed cut the federal funds target rate to between 0.0% and 0.25%, and President Bush announced that the government would invest TARP funds in GM and Chrysler.

In spite of this kitchen-sink assortment of remedies, however, the broader financial markets remained in a panicked state though the end of the year and into early 2009. Table V.8 shows the trend of the S&P 500 from the end of August 2008 through the rest of the year.

As this table shows, the S&P started September 2008 at 1,283, plunged about 30% by the end of November, and then held at about this level as it closed out December.

Although not shown in the chart, the index continued its descent in the first two months of 2009, and by the end of February, it was at 735. This was a stunning 43% decline from where it had been at the beginning of September, just before Lehman failed.

The S&P 500: August 2008 to December 2008   Table V.8

Source of underlying data: Yahoo Finance

		S&P 500 at End of Month	Pct. Change from August	
Last month of Stress Stage				
2008	August	1,283		
Panic Stage				
2008	September	1,166	-9%	*In the aftermath of Lehman's failure,*
	October	969	-24%	*the authorities rolled out a myriad of*
	November	896	-30%	*interventions, none of which led to*
	December	903	-30%	*a recovery – the S&P 500 remained depressed through the end of the year.*

The TED had averaged 131 bps during the Stress stage of the crisis (November 2007 through August 2008) and was a bit below this in the months leading up to Lehman's failure. Then, in October 2008, it averaged an otherworldly 335 bps, before dropping to the still-stratospheric levels of 210 bps in November and 180 bps in December. This downward trend from the October peak may indicate that the myriad of programs rolled out by the authorities were somewhat helpful in keeping the short-term financing markets from spinning even further out of control. It is also possible, however, that the improvements in this index reflected a growing sense that the authorities had learned their lesson from Lehman's failure and were not about to drop another "Lehman surprise" on the markets.

Nevertheless, both the TED and the S&P show that the financial markets remained in a state of severe panic as 2008 came to a close. The vast "bailout sink" response may have helped keep things from getting even worse, but it did *not* end the panic.

RESOLVING THE PANIC

While it would have been hard for the authorities to discern amidst the post-Lehman confusion, the benefit of hindsight makes it clear that the primary concerns roiling the financial markets during the Panic stage of the crisis boiled down to a handful of critical institutions. Once it became clear that none of these entities would become "another Lehman," the panic in the market subsided, and a sustained recovery ensued shortly thereafter.

In the immediate aftermath of Lehman's failure, the critically endangered firms included the three surviving major investment banks: Merrill Lynch, Morgan Stanley, and Goldman Sachs. In addition, the markets were acutely concerned about Citigroup because of its highly leveraged balance sheet and its direct and indirect (through "off-balance-sheet" guarantees) exposure to mortgages. And finally, markets were on high alert about Bank of America, which had acquired the giant subprime lender Countrywide in July and was under contract to acquire Merrill Lynch.

As will be further detailed in Part VI, Morgan Stanley and Goldman Sachs were in a much better position to withstand the panic than were Bear Stearns, Lehman, and Merrill. Both Morgan and Goldman were able to complete private capital raisings during the early part of the Panic stage, which had two beneficial effects. First, it further shored up their capacity to weather the downturn in housing prices. Second, it signaled to the broader financial markets that substantial private investors *believed* these investment banks were capable of surviving the crisis.

While Goldman and Morgan were in relatively strong financial shape even before their fundraisings, Merrill's tangible stockholders' equity relative to its mortgage exposure was much closer to where Bear and Lehman had been before they reached the point of failure. This obviously made Merrill a prime focus of concern, which Merrill itself was well aware of. It is fair to conclude that this is why Merrill's executives had agreed to a distressed sale to BofA. Indeed, the agreement to sell Merrill to BofA was hammered out over the same weekend that the authorities decided that Lehman would not be bailed out.

While BofA's pending purchase initially helped alleviate market concerns about Merrill, escalating mortgage problems at Merrill during the remainder of the year would later cause BofA to consider invoking the material adverse change (MAC) clause in their purchase agreement. This would have enabled BofA to back out of the transaction but also would have left Merrill dangling at the discretion of the authorities, much as Lehman had been in September. As I will show, the resolution of the uncertainty over BofA's willingness and ability to absorb Merrill's problems would become the final clearing point for the resolution of the panic, but markets did not cross this bridge until after concerns about Citigroup had been put to a somewhat incestuous bed.

Citigroup

Citigroup's problems were an especially delicate matter for the authorities involved. For one, Robert Rubin, former secretary of the treasury and a member (along with Alan Greenspan and Larry Summers) of *Time*'s "Committee to Save the World," had been a high-profile and highly compensated member of Citi's board of directors since 1999. Moreover, Tim Geithner, Rubin's former protégé at the Treasury Department, had been president of the Federal Reserve Bank of New York since 2003. On top of all this, the Federal Reserve had primary regulatory responsibility for Citigroup, and this responsibility was handled by the New York branch that Geithner oversaw.

If the authorities allowed Citi to fail, as they had done with Lehman, it would have been enormously embarrassing, and perhaps even politically devastating, for the reputations of Rubin, Geithner, and the Federal Reserve. On the other hand, if Citi was seen as receiving special treatment because of either Rubin's political connections or the Fed's desire to protect its own reputation, the authorities would have come under intense scrutiny for bestowing favors on one organization that had not been extended to a less politically connected firm (Lehman).

One way for the authorities to have a bailout and disguise it too was to arrange a mass bailout package for a wide array of firms, including many that did *not* need such assistance to survive. This would be my interpretation of the highly publicized meeting that the Fed and the Treasury conducted with nine large financial firms in mid-October, about a month after Lehman's failure, to inform them that they had been selected for what was officially called the Capital Purchase Program (CPP) but was effectively the first step in a thinly disguised, multistage bailout of Citigroup.

News of the CPP, and of the authorities' expectation that all nine of the selected financial firms would participate in the program, was delivered to the firms at a tense meeting on October 14, 2008, about a month after Lehman's failure. Sheila Bair, then head of the FDIC, was in attendance and later reported, "All of the invitees had been hand picked by Tim Geithner. And, as I had just learned... the game plan for the meeting was for Hank [Paulson, secretary of the treasury] to tell all those CEOs that they would have to accept government capital investments in their institutions, at least temporarily."[9]

As Ms. Bair also observed, "The investment banks were in trouble, but Merrill had arranged to sell itself to BofA, and Goldman and Morgan had been able to raise new capital from private sources, with the capacity, I believed, to raise more if necessary. Without government aid, some of them might have had to forgo bonuses and take losses for several quarters, but still, it seemed to me that they were strong enough to bumble through."[10]

Based on the analysis of the investment banks to be presented in Part VI and on the private capital raisings completed by Goldman and Morgan after Lehman's collapse, I agree with Ms. Bair's assessment of the investment banks: Goldman and Morgan were capable of surviving *without* the CPP funds, while Merrill was in trouble and in need of funds, but its sale to BofA had, at that time, presumably alleviated concerns about Merrill.

The remaining six institutions were all commercial banks. As Ms. Bair noted with respect to these institutions, "The fact remained that with the exception of Citi, the commercial banks' capital levels seemed to be adequate.... Citi probably did need that kind of massive government assistance (indeed, it would need two more bailouts later on), but there was the rub. How much of the decision making was being driven through the prism of the special needs of that one, politically connected, institution?"[11]

Ms. Bair also noted that she was not the only one to observe that the authorities' response to the crisis seemed to have been designed at least in part to mask Citi's problems: Warren Buffett, for example, "was quoted in the *Financial Times* complaining that Citigroup's high-profile problems had tainted the entire industry."[12]

THE CRITICAL FINANCIAL INSTITUTIONS

As I have already noted, in spite of all the kitchen-sink-like bailout activity following Lehman's failure, I believe the real concerns in the market boiled down to three firms: Citigroup, Merrill Lynch, and, in part because of its pending acquisition of Merrill, Bank of America. Let's now look at the evidence showing that once fears surrounding these financial giants were finally put to bed, the panicked conditions in the market soon subsided.

Of the nine firms called into the tense CPP meeting in mid-October, the Fed and the Treasury had decided that Citigroup would receive $25 billion, which was about two-thirds more than the next largest capital infusions announced at the meeting. The three other large commercial banks—Wells Fargo, J.P. Morgan Chase, and Bank of America—were each allocated $15 billion. The three investment banks—Goldman, Morgan, and Merrill—were allocated $10 billion each, and the two commercial banks that also benefited from their large transaction servicing businesses—Bank of New York and State Street—received $3 billion and $2 billion, respectively.

Even though Citigroup received a much larger infusion than any of the other firms, its dire problems would soon force it back for another helping at the bailout trough. As George Harrison and the Beatles might have said, "Have you seen the bigger piggies in their starched white shirts? You will find the bigger piggies stirring up the dirt, always have clean shirts to play around in."[13]

In mid-November it was announced that Citi would receive an additional $20 billion of capital *and* that the Fed had agreed to provide what came to be known as a "ring-fence" backstop that limited Citi's exposure to losses on $306 billion of problem residential and commercial mortgage securities in its portfolio. If the initial $25 billion bailout announced in October wasn't enough to quell market fears over real and perceived risks at Citi, the additional $20 billion plus the "ring-fence" made it clear that the authorities were simply *not* going to let Citi become another "Lehman surprise."

In spite of Citi's bailout, the markets remained panicked through December. Something else was still causing high levels of market consternation—and that something was the uncertainty surrounding BofA's acquisition of Merrill.

Bank of America and Merrill Lynch

Even after the shareholders of both companies approved the merger on December 5, 2008, BofA's acquisition of Merrill was still percolating as something of a "damned if they do, damned if they don't" pot of problems.

If BofA completed the acquisition, Merrill (as a subsidiary of the commercial bank) would benefit from BofA's more robust balance sheet and financing options, and would therefore no longer be directly dependent on the panicked capital markets for short-term financing. This was all to the good for Merrill. At the same time, however, markets were concerned that if the deal was consummated, BofA itself might be unable to survive the combination of its own mortgage issues, those it acquired with Countrywide in July, *and* Merrill's problems.

If, on the other hand, BofA walked away from the transaction, as it was considering, then the bank would not have to deal with Merrill's mortgage problems, which would be positive for BofA. But in this scenario, Merrill's survival would be left to the panicked markets and the discretion of the same authorities that had chosen to let Lehman fail under similar circumstances.

All of which would obviously be quite embarrassing for the authorities. If BofA didn't solve their Merrill problem, how would they explain providing the kind of bailout package to one investment bank (Merrill) that they had failed to provide to another (Lehman)? If BofA canceled the acquisition of Merrill and the authorities chose to let Merrill fail, as they had done with Lehman, there was a risk of sending the market even deeper into dysfunction. From this perspective, it was clearly very much in the authorities' interest to have BofA complete the acquisition, *whether it wanted to or not.*

Indeed, nervousness over all of this was not limited to the financial markets. Bernanke later recounted how he and Hank Paulson, the secretary of the treasury, responded to hearing that Bank of America's CEO, Ken Lewis, was wavering on the merger: "Paulson and I had been relieved at Merrill's apparent stabilization, so we were shaken to learn in mid-December that the deal was threatening to come undone.... Lewis told us that Bank of America had only recently determined that Merrill was likely to suffer much greater than anticipated losses in the fourth quarter (it would eventually announce a $15.3 billion loss). Lewis said he was considering invoking a clause in the contract with Merrill—known as a material adverse change clause, or MAC clause."[14]

Obviously, it would be something of an understatement to say that Bernanke and Paulson both pushed hard for Lewis to go forward with the transaction and also gave assurances that the authorities would provide additional bailout support if BofA closed on the deal. As Bernanke described these tense developments, "Hank and I did make clear that we thought that invoking the MAC clause was a terrible idea for both Bank of America and the financial system. We also told him what we had already said publicly: We would do what was necessary to prevent any more failures of systemically important financial institutions."[15]

Following the discussions with the authorities, Lewis and BofA's board decided to move forward with the merger, which was completed on New Year's Day of 2009.

BofA's decision to consummate the merger removed Merrill from the hot seat of market concerns, but it still left BofA exposed to both the problems in Merrill's mortgage portfolio and its own mortgage issues. As Bernanke acknowledged, "Merrill's losses were large and Lewis had reason to be concerned about the stability of the combined companies, particularly because Bank of America had substantial losses of its own."[16]

The solution was for the authorities to arrange another round of bailout financing modeled on the November deal for Citigroup. In this case, Bank of America received an additional $20 billion in direct funding from the Treasury's Toxic Asset Relief Program (TARP), while the Treasury, the Fed, and the FDIC agreed to a "ring-fence" backstop on $118 billion of BofA's problem loans, most of which had been acquired in the Merrill deal.

The BofA-Merrill bailout package was announced on January 16, 2009.

THE PANIC COMES TO AN END

The markets had been in a state of deep confusion and panic for nearly four months following Lehman's failure, and no one had set forth a laundry list with the Bank of America bailout as the last item to be checked off before a recovery could begin. It took a short while for the broader financial markets to recognize that the January 16 bailout of BofA effectively ended any danger that another "Lehman surprise" would roil the system. The S&P declined for about another month and a half after the bailout of BofA. The index reached a low weekly close at the end of the first week of March, and then began a powerful recovery.

Let's now trace the TED spread through the resolution of the concerns about Merrill and BofA. Several key steps were taken toward alleviating marketplace fears that one of these two firms could become another Lehman: The first of these steps was the vote by shareholders on December 5, 2008 to approve BofA's acquisition of Merrill. Second was the pressure on Ken Lewis from Bernanke and Paulson in late December as they "strongly advised" Bank of America's CEO to go forward with the deal and also reassured him that they intended to live up to their public promises not to let any more critical firms fail. The third key step was BofA's decision to consummate the acquisition on January 1, 2009. And the final critical step was the announcement of the bailout package for BofA on January 16.

As these steps built one upon the other, the TED gradually descended from its stratospheric post-Lehman levels back down to where it had been before the interbank lending markets went into panic mode. This descent is reflected in Table V.9.

The TED averaged 210 bps during the month of November 2008 and 216 bps in the week ending on Friday, December 5, the day that the shareholders of both Merrill and BofA approved the merger. Two

The TED Spread: November 2008 to January 2009   **Table V.9**

Source of underlying data: Federal Reserve Bank of St. Louis

	Key Events	Average TED Spread	
November 2008			
Avg. for Month		210	
December 2008	For weekly period ending on Friday		
12/05	BofA / Merrill shareholders approve merger	216	*The TED spread was still at Panic levels, but then began to decline with BofA's shareholder approval of the Merrill purchase.*
12/12		206	
12/19	Bernanke / Paulson strongly advise BofA not to invoke MAC*	163	*The spread declined further as the authorities: 1) pressured BofA's CEO not to invoke the MAC clause, and 2) provided assurance that a bailout package would be forthcoming if the merger was consummated.*
12/26		146	
January 2009			
01/02	BofA consummates merger	135	
01/09		126	
01/16	Bailout package for BofA announced	100	*The week the bailout package was announced, the spread dropped significantly. It continued to register at pre-Panic levels for the first time since Lehman's failure.*
01/23		103	
01/30		99	

* MAC = Material Adverse Consequences clause. In light of the escalating mortgage write-downs at Merrill, BofA was considering invoking the clause to back out of its previous agreement to acquire Merrill

weeks after the merger approval, the TED was down to 163, and it dropped again to 146 during the last week ending in December. This was the period when Bernanke and Paulson were urging Lewis to complete the deal and providing assurances that they would work to deliver whatever bailout support was needed to ensure that the combined firm would not fail.

Lewis and BofA's board consummated the merger on Thursday, January 1, and the TED averaged 135 bps for the week, down slightly from the average for the week before.

The bailout package providing the final assurances that BofA/Merrill would not fail became official with a public announcement on Friday, January 16, at which point the TED was down to 100 bps, less than half of where it had been in early December before this chain of events unfolded to its ultimate resolution.

In the four weeks before Lehman failed (from mid-August to mid-September 2008), the TED averaged 111 bps. In the four weeks after the BofA bailout package, the TED averaged 97 bps, and it did not rise above the pre-Lehman average again. Just as it had throughout the crisis, the TED reacted a bit more quickly to these developments than did the S&P, but the two measures charted a similar course.

With the resolution of all remaining issues surrounding BofA and Merrill on January 16, 2009, the Panic stage of the crisis was effectively over. The resolution of the panic was reflected in the short-term lending markets almost immediately, though it would take a little longer to register in the broader financial markets. In other words: the mid-January bailout of BofA/Merrill represented the fat lady's final aria, after which the more seasoned and attentive operagoers in the front seats promptly headed for the exits. The less experienced spectators in the back rows were caught dozing, but soon awoke to an empty theater and thereafter departed as well.

-26-

RECOVERY

iven the remarkable levels of panic after Lehman's collapse, it is not surprising that the broader financial markets took a bit longer than the TED to grasp that the bailout of BofA on January 16, 2009 effectively ended any risk of another "Lehman surprise" with respect to any of the other critical financial institutions. Once this realization took hold, however, the recovery in the S&P 500 was sudden, robust, and sustained.

The low weekly close for the S&P was 683 at the end of the week of March 2, 2009. From there, the index shot up over 20% to close out March at 843, and then the increases continued at a generally steady clip through December. The S&P ended the year up roughly 50% from its low point in early March. In fact, the recovery was so strong that the S&P closed out 2009 at 1,115, just 13% below where it had been at the beginning of September 2008, before Lehman's failure.

By contrast, the recovery reflected in the TED spread occurred in two stages.

The first stage consisted of the steady drop in the TED recounted above as the BofA/Merrill merger and bailout proceeded to resolution. As noted earlier, the TED dropped down to 100 bps for the week ending January 16, 2009, when BofA's bailout package was announced. This was actually *below* the TED's four-week average just before Lehman's failure. It then hovered around 100 bps for the next three months before starting another gradual descent that eventually brought it down to 25 bps in August, where it basically remained for the rest of the year. This was the second stage of the recovery in the short-term lending markets.

Some have claimed that the key to ending the crisis was the stress tests that the Fed conducted on many financial institutions. The analysis here demonstrates otherwise: the upturn in the S&P began in March 2009, well before the results of the stress tests were released on May 7. Obviously, the stress tests did not spark the powerful recovery in the broader financial markets. On the other hand, while the TED had dropped back to pre-Lehman levels in January, it remained in a stressed state until around the time that the tests were released. This indicates that the stress tests likely did help bring interbank lending markets back down to pre-crisis levels later in the year.

The main value of the stress tests, however, was in revealing that the vast majority of the financial system was actually in good health even through the Panic stage of the crisis. This is consistent with the conclusion that, as Sheila Bair also observed, the real issue during this time boiled down to a handful of critical firms.

-27-

SUMMARY

The Liftoff of the housing bubble in 1998 was triggered by the aggressive expansion of the GSEs, and the Acceleration that began in 2002 was driven by the easy-money policies of the Federal Reserve. As the housing bubble pushed home prices to unprecedented levels, mortgage debt outstanding soared to 72% of GDP in 2006. This left a number of the nation's largest financial institutions systemically exposed to single-family home loans whose values depended on the precarious housing values created by the policies at the GSEs and their federal overseers and at the Fed.

Because of both the GSEs' accounting problems and the soaring demand for adjustable-rate financing spurred by the Fed's easy-money policy, Wall Street investment banks and other financial institutions—such as Citigroup, BofA, and other commercial banks—had stepped in to finance the surge in mortgage demand during the Acceleration phase of the bubble. Even though Wall Street was in the business of securitizing and selling mortgages, not holding them for investment, the investment banks still needed to hold sizable mortgage positions to facilitate their securitizations. The systemic exposure to mortgages of dubious value at a number of the nation's largest financial institutions is what differentiated the failure of Lehman Brothers from the long list of Wall Street failures that had occurred over the prior century, none of which had sparked anything like the panic that followed Lehman's failure.

The financial markets became aware of emerging problems with declining mortgage values in July and August of 2007 when hedge funds managed by Bear Stearns and BNP Paribas announced severe losses and suspended redemptions. This brought a halt to the upward trend of the S&P 500, but the broader markets then stabilized—until a wave of fourth-quarter write-downs and losses, along with some dismissals of prominent CEOs, put the S&P on a downward trend and heightened the stress in the interbank lending markets.

The dire announcements continued in early 2008, which led to steepening losses in the S&P 500. Then, remarkably, the markets turned and actually rebounded after Bear Stearns reached the point of failure in early March. I believe that this otherwise inexplicable upturn in the S&P amidst the darkening skies of the housing collapse is a clear indicator that the markets took Bear's rescue as a sign that the Fed would continue to backstop the system in order to prevent a severe downturn, just as the Fed (and "the Committee to Save the World") had done in various ways since the 1987 stock market crash.

In July, the authorities agreed to invoke emergency provisions to bail out the GSEs, even though they were, as later events demonstrated, insolvent at the time. Likewise, AIG was clearly insolvent when it was rescued the day after Lehman failed, but the authorities used a going-concern valuation to justify this bailout.

Even if the authorities were spot-on in these judgments, it is hard to see how market participants could have been anything but confused by the decision to let Lehman fail after the smorgasbord of justifications that had been given for saving other critical financial institutions over a span of twenty years. There is no greater proof that markets had expected Lehman to be backstopped than the gut-wrenching drop in the S&P and the stratospheric levels of the TED that followed Lehman's demise. If the markets weren't caught completely off guard by the decision to let Lehman fail, then how else are these reactions to be explained? Contrary to what the authorities themselves later asserted, I believe that they could have chosen to bail out Lehman if given sufficient political backing, and that such a step would have averted the Panic stage of the crisis.

After deciding not to bail out Lehman, the authorities then responded to the resulting panic by throwing something of a bailout sink at the financial system, rolling out one program after another. Nevertheless, the high levels of panic reflected in both the S&P and the TED through the end of the year provide convincing evidence that this approach, while likely helpful in some ways, did not address the real source of fear in the marketplace.

Feeling once burned and twice shy, markets weren't looking for blanket promises. Rather, if the markets were going to continue to finance the remaining critical firms whose survival might become dependent on the discretion of the authorities, they wanted first to see that the authorities had arranged and committed specific bailout funds for these critical firms. The worries mostly revolved around three institutions: Citigroup, Merrill Lynch, and Bank of America. Once sufficient bailout packages for these firms were formally committed to and announced, the Panic stage of the crisis quickly came to an end.

The Panic stage ended well before the results of the stress tests were made public in May 2009. This does not mean the stress tests were a bad idea. In fact, they were valuable in showing that the overall financial system was in generally sound condition except for a few critical firms. This is consistent with the idea that much of the post-Lehman bailout policy was designed to hide the embarrassing and potentially politically damaging failure of the Fed's regulatory responsibility for Citigroup. It also supports the thesis that the key to ending the crisis was the resolution of the problems at a small handful of critical institutions.

The panic resulting from the failure of Lehman Brothers in mid-September 2008 lasted about four to six months, depending on whether we locate the endpoint in mid-January 2009, when the bailout of BofA/Merrill occurred and the TED spread dropped back down to pre-Lehman stress levels, or in early March, when the dazed S&P picked up on the significance of the BofA bailout and took off toward what by year's end would be a 60%+ recovery from its earlier low weekly close.

PART VI

INVESTMENT BANKS, MONEY MARKET FUNDS, AND ALTERNATIVE THEORIES OF THE CRISIS

-28-

PREVIEW

believe the analysis set forth above demonstrates that the underlying cause of the financial crisis was the housing bubble, which was initially triggered by the GSEs and then blown to even more dangerous proportions by the Federal Reserve. Nevertheless, the idea that the more lightly regulated investment banks were responsible for the crisis took on a life of its own in the aftermath of the Panic stage. A number of allegations regarding the investment banks' culpability seemed to take hold apparently without anyone bothering to check the underlying facts. For example, some alleged that the under-regulated investment banks dangerously increased their leverage in the years leading up to the panic. Others asserted that the use of derivatives was to blame. And still others blamed their eventual problems on an overreliance on short-term funding sources. I will show that each of these beliefs is inconsistent with the actual data.

In order to separate fact from fiction, I have combined and analyzed the publicly filed financial statements of the major investment banks. One of the most important conclusions drawn from this analysis has to do with what, in my opinion, actually did cause some banks to fail while others survived. Understanding what I have called this "critical measure" provides important lessons to help corporate overseers navigate future panics.

This section also includes a discussion of money market mutual funds' role in the financial crisis. While such funds did not cause the crisis, they did have the potential to make it much worse. The financial panic exposed underlying flaws in the structure of the money markets, which will be explained below. Unfortunately, these flaws were only partially addressed by subsequent regulations.

Finally, we'll examine a number of alternative theories about the cause of the crisis including: that it resulted from gradual deregulation, or from a so-called "global savings glut," or from other fundamental factors, such as building costs and home affordability, that could have been the cause. As I will show, none of these alternative theories provides a supportable explanation of the crisis.

-29-

THE INVESTMENT BANKS

We saw earlier how the Fed reacted to the collapse of the tech stock bubble in 2000 by dramatically lowering short-term interest rates. This had a twofold impact on the housing bubble.

First, the Fed's actions pushed the interest rate on variable-rate mortgages below the level of nominal home appreciation, thereby creating enormous incentives for homebuyers to finance purchases with adjustable-rate mortgages. As a consequence, ARM origination rose nearly 200% during the Acceleration phase (2002–2005) of the housing bubble.

Second, the Fed's artificially low interest rates also caused a scramble by investors seeking to earn acceptable returns on their savings, which sparked demand for investments generating higher yields than those available on other, traditional, money market securities.

The combination of these factors helped fuel mortgage securitizations, which may sound complicated but are essentially just legal vehicles formed to hold mortgages so that the interest and principal payments made on these assets can be passed through to the investors who own securities in such vehicles. Much has been made of the complexity of the mortgage securities created by Wall Street during this period and of the poor job the rating agencies often did in assessing these securities. Whatever merits these criticisms may have, I think it is safe to say that neither complexity nor the rating agencies caused the financial crisis. Rather, the panic occurred because the bubble led to systemic mortgage exposure and the unexpected failure of Lehman Brothers caused the capital markets to lose confidence that policymakers would back other systemically exposed institutions.

Critical financial institutions from across the regulatory spectrum—the GSEs, major commercial banks like Citigroup, and the investment banks—were *all* involved in the securitization markets. But the massive growth of mortgage securitization brought the investment banks into housing finance in a significant way for the first time during the housing bubble. Then, the failures of Bear Stearns and Lehman Brothers—both of which marked prominent turning points in the financial crisis—brought high levels of public scrutiny onto the investment banks.

The Occupy Wall Street protests that came later were a prominent symbol of public outrage over the sense of unfairness that selected Wall Street "fat cats" and institutions were bailed out while many working-class citizens lost their homes, jobs, and savings. Furthermore, because the investment banks were the least heavily regulated of the critical firms in the eye of the crisis, the idea that the investment banks caused the problems fit nicely with the narrative that the crisis was somehow a result of underregulated greed. Adding to the sense of intrigue and suspicion resulting from all of this, Wall Street was also lumped into the nebulous world of the so-called "shadow banking system."

THE SHADOW BANKING SYSTEM

While the term "shadow banking system" has an ominous, borderline-illegal feel to it, in reality it simply refers to the migration of lending activities away from deposit-funded institutions (like banks or savings and loans) and toward other sources of capital such as money market mutual funds and securitization markets, including the one for mortgages that played a role in the financial crisis.

Before the development of the shadow banking system, a large corporate borrower would likely have turned to a commercial bank for a loan. In such a case, the commercial bank would have lent the corporation funds that were sourced largely from the bank's depositors. This all started to change with the advent of securitized lending in the 1970s.

While it sounds complicated, and can become so in practice, at a conceptual level securitized lending is no more complex than selling common stock in a company or forming a partnership to buy a rental property. In a securitized loan transaction, a package of usually similar loans is placed in a legal entity, and then securities that represent a claim on the income and principal payments from the loans are created and sold directly to investors. Because securitization transactions like this had the effect of removing the banks from their intermediary role between the source of funds (the saver, who previously deposited his funds in the bank's accounts) and the borrower (the corporation), the whole process is often referred to as "disintermediation."

While often left out of the discussion of the shadow banking markets, the GSEs were also a significant source of disintermediation out of the traditional deposit-based system for home mortgage loans. Indeed, as noted earlier, the GSEs' share of the single-family mortgage market rose from less than 12% in 1975 to around 50% by the mid-2000s.

In addition, the GSEs also played a pioneering role in the process of securitizing single-family mortgages. In fact, by 2002, over half of Fannie Mae's combined book of business consisted of mortgage-backed securities that it had sold to investors. These securities were still considered to be a part of Fannie's overall book of business because Fannie continued to receive fees in exchange for providing guarantees against the risk of principal loss on the mortgages that had been securitized and sold.

As was chronicled previously, the aggressive growth of the GSEs triggered and drove the Liftoff phase (1998–2001) of the housing bubble. Because of both their accounting misdeeds and the Fed's rate policies in the early 2000s, however, the GSEs then took a passenger seat during the Acceleration phase (2002–2005) of the bubble. To be clear, the GSEs grew rapidly during Acceleration, but they were no longer leading the charge.

When the GSEs were pushed out of the driver's seat of the housing bubble in the early 2000s, Wall Street stepped in to benefit from the securitization opportunities resulting from the mortgage demand spurred by the Fed's low interest rates. And even though Wall Street was in the business of packaging and selling mortgage securities (as opposed to holding mortgages for the income they produced), the investment banks still needed to inventory home mortgage assets on their books in order to expedite their securitization businesses. Many of these assets, somewhat ironically, were the highly rated (and lower-yielding) pieces of securitizations that became harder and harder to sell as investors desperately searched for higher yields in the low-rate environment engineered by the Fed.

In other words, the Fed's low-rate policies had the dual effect of creating high levels of demand from homebuyers for short-term adjustable-rate mortgages, and simultaneously leading to elevated levels of demand from savers seeking higher yields on their investments—all of which pushed mortgage securitizations ever upward. The systemic exposure to mortgage securities with values that were endangered by the then-unknown magnitude of the looming collapse of the bubble is what set the financial panic of 2008 apart from the many times in the past when investment banks had failed *without* jeopardizing market confidence in the rest of the financial system.

Fortunately, all five of the major investment banks in the eye of the financial storm—Bear Stearns, Lehman Brothers, Merrill Lynch, Morgan Stanley, and Goldman Sachs—were public companies, which means they all filed publicly available financial reports throughout the buildup to the crisis. In order to better understand Wall Street's behavior during those years, I have combined and analyzed their annual reports from 1999 through 2007. This analysis yields important information about the investment banks such as the level of leverage they employed, their use of derivative securities, their reliance on short-term funding sources, and other matters. In addition, it also reveals what I believe was the critical measure that separated the investment banks that were capable of surviving on their own from those that required bailouts to survive.

ASSET ANALYSIS

Let's begin our analysis of the five major investment banks by looking at growth in what I will call combined "adjusted total assets," which equals reported total assets less goodwill and intangibles, positions that net out, and variable-interest entities. This will help assess whether the firms were growing at reckless or manageable rates as they expanded their mortgage securitization businesses.

Goodwill and intangibles have been eliminated because they often arise out of acquisition accounting and because—unlike cash, securities, or other properties—they generally have no liquidation value to support creditors or equity holders in a worst-case scenario. In panicked conditions, investors tend to ignore the book value of such intangible assets in assessing a financial institution's ability to meet its obligations.

Positions that net out have been eliminated because they involve assets and liabilities that offset one another, usually in the same amount. Often arising from securities lending and borrowing transactions, these positions usually involve counterparties who are looking to the offsetting securities values as collateral for their position, not the overall financial health of the organization that the counterparties have provided funds to.

Finally, variable-interest entities have also been eliminated. These are vehicles like partnerships that are sponsored by a company that then manages the assets of the partnership on behalf of other investors. In such vehicles, the sponsoring company typically holds a minority stake but has limited exposure to the losses of the underlying partnership. In the wake of the Enron collapse, the accounting regulations required that many such entities be included on the sponsor's books even though doing so often created the misleading appearance that the sponsoring entity owned assets that really belonged to others and was responsible for liabilities that were really just obligations of the underlying partnership.

I have made these adjustments in order to get a better picture of the true economic assets and liabilities of the major investment banks during the period under study—a picture that is closer to how a sophisticated market investor would assess the economic viability of these organizations under stressed conditions.

Total Asset Growth Rates

Table VI.1 presents combined adjusted total assets for the five major investment banks from 1999 through 2006.

The first point of interest in this table is that the adjusted combined total assets of the five major investment banks grew from about $1.3 billion in 1999 to about $3.5 billion in 2006. This works out to a compounded rate of growth for the seven-year period of a

The Major Investment Banks: Growth in Adjusted Total Assets   **Table VI.1**

Source of underlying data: Company Annual Reports

		Adjusted Total Assets	Growth Rate
1999		1,263,318	
2000		1,505,553	19%
2001		1,620,540	8%
2002		1,734,310	7%
2003	*Acceleration*	1,951,545	13%
2004	*Phase*	2,447,451	25%
2005		2,858,698	17%
2006	*Deceleration*	3,488,326	22%
Average			**16%**

From '99 to '06, the major investment banks grew at an average rate of 16%.

bit under 16% per year. To be sure, this was a fast rate of growth, but nowhere near the kind of breakneck pace that we might have expected given the ultimate fate of these organizations. Indeed, the growth rate exceeded 20% in only two years and never went above 25%.

All in all, this information presents a picture of firms that grew at a rapid but manageable pace during this period.

Growth Rates by Asset Type

Next, I have broken down each firm's assets into three categories, to see if there were any significant shifts in the balance of assets owned that might have served as a red flag to managers or regulators.

For lack of a better term, I'll call the first category "business assets" simply because these are assets that are incidental to the daily operation of the investment banking business. Assets lumped together here include: cash, deposits at banks, segregated securities, receivables, property, and other.

The second category includes assets involved in securities financing transactions. The primary assets here are securities sold under agreements to repurchase and securities borrowed.

The Major Investment Banks: Asset Allocations　　　　　　　**Table VI.2**

Source of underlying data: Company Annual Reports

		Business Assets	Securities Finance Assets	Trading and Investment Assets	Total Adjusted Assets	
1999		21%	43%	36%	100%	The mix of assets at the major investment banks remained relatively stable throughout the Acceleration phase as well. Trading and investment assets, which includes mortgages and real estate investments, held steady at around 41% of adjusted assets throughout the Acceleration.
2000		24%	39%	37%	100%	
2001		22%	38%	39%	100%	
2002		20%	40%	41%	100%	
2003	Acceleration	20%	38%	42%	100%	
2004	Phase	20%	40%	39%	100%	
2005		18%	43%	39%	100%	
2006	Deceleration	18%	41%	41%	100%	
Average		20%	40%	39%	100%	

The final category consists of trading and investments. These are assets that are either traded or held for profit and include the mortgage and other real estate positions held by these firms.

Let's now take a look at how these three asset categories evolved over the course of the bubble.

What I find most interesting in Table VI.2 is the relative stability of Wall Street's asset mixture during this period. True, trading assets and investments did grow some from 1999 to 2006 (increasing from 36% of total assets at the beginning of the period to 41% at the end), but not by an extraordinary amount.

Perhaps most importantly, there was no increase in the percentage of trading assets from 2002 forward. This means that all of the expansion in the relative share of Wall Street's holdings of trading assets and investments occurred *before* the Acceleration phase of the bubble, which is when the Wall Street firms were most involved in underwriting the securitizations that helped finance the escalation of the housing bubble during this period.

The lack of obvious red flags in the analysis of overall growth and asset composition should give pause to those who believe that

The Major Investment Banks: Derivative Assets **Table VI.3**

Source of underlying data: Company Annual Reports

		Derivatives as % of Total Adjusted Assets	
1999		7.2%	
2000		6.8%	
2001		7.4%	
2002		8.2%	
2003	Acceleration	7.8%	
2004	Phase	8.0%	
2005		5.7%	*Derivative use remained relatively constant,*
2006	Deceleration	5.5%	*and actually trended down in 2005 and '06.*
Average		7.1%	

more intense regulatory oversight would have led to restrictions that could have curtailed the housing bubble.

Derivatives

Derivative exposure also received a great deal of attention in connection with the financial crisis. One prominent theory was that the use of derivatives increased dangerously and that such derivatives were like weapons of financial mass destruction lurking in Wall Street's shadowy corridors. Because derivative holdings were disclosed as a part of trading assets and investments, we can take a look at combined derivative assets as a percentage of adjusted total assets during the housing bubble.

As Table VI.3 shows, derivative assets actually *declined* somewhat over the course of the bubble. Such assets represented 7.2% of combined adjusted total assets in 1999 but dropped to 5.5% by 2006. Again, no red flags appear in this analysis of Wall Street's use of derivatives.

Mortgage and Real Estate Assets

Finally, we'll look at mortgage and real estate assets as a percentage of combined adjusted total assets. Because Morgan Stanley did not

The Major Investment Banks: Mortgage & Real Estate Assets

Table VI.4

Source of underlying data: Company Annual Reports

		Mortgage and Real Estate as % of Total Adjusted Assets*	
1999		4.9%	
2000		7.4%	
2001		10.3%	
2002		11.2%	*Mortgage and Real Estate assets grew from '99–'02, but then remained relatively constant as a percentage of total adjusted assets during the Acceleration phase and declined slightly during the Deceleration.*
2003	Acceleration	11.3%	
2004	Phase	11.1%	
2005		11.3%	
2006	Deceleration	10.7%	
Average		9.8%	

* This table excludes Morgan Stanley, which did not separately report mortgage holdings until 2007.

separately disclose its mortgage holdings until 2007, their financials have been excluded from the data in Table VI.4.

Interestingly, we can see that mortgage and real estate assets as a share of combined total adjusted assets (excluding Morgan Stanley) grew from about 5% in 1999 to over 11% in 2002, and then held relatively constant thereafter, even declining a bit in 2006. Once again, even knowing that a dangerous housing bubble developed during this time, this hardly paints a picture of a set of companies carelessly careening toward their inevitable demise—which should give pause to those who believe that regulators or other overseers would be able to identify similar dangers in the future.

We will soon come to an analysis that I believe highlights exactly what ultimately scared the financial markets regarding these firms. For now, I believe it is safe to say that this review of the assets of the investment banks does *not* present the picture of obviously self-destructive practices that we might have expected given the ultimate fate of these organizations and much of the condemning narrative that arose around them.

Nor is the lack of obviously reckless behavior surprising. Why? Because the executives of many of these firms—including Bear Stearns and Lehman Brothers—held large amounts of stock in these organizations and therefore had much to lose if they failed. As Warren Buffett might have observed, "the execs were eating their own cooking." Obviously this didn't prevent them from making serious mistakes, but they had strong incentives to manage their organizations prudently.

LIABILITY ANALYSIS

In order to look at the investment banks' use of leverage and other potential red flags, I have also made the corresponding adjustments and eliminations described earlier—for intangibles, offsetting liabilities, and variable interest entities—to the data on liabilities and stockholders' equity. Most importantly, intangibles have been eliminated from stockholders' equity to arrive at tangible stockholders' equity, a much more conservative and better measure of strength in a storm than the full GAAP (Generally Accepted Accounting Principles) presentation of stockholders' equity. Unless otherwise noted, the following data refers to the combined financial statements of all five major investment banks.

Tangible Stockholders' Equity

A common contemporary perception of the financial crisis was that Wall Street engaged in a dangerous game of leveraging itself up as it gorged on the mortgage assets that eventually caused it to choke. We have already seen that this allegation does not square with the analysis of their assets presented above.

Let's now look at tangible stockholders' equity (TSE) as a percentage of adjusted total assets in order to get a better picture of whether Wall Street collectively leveraged up its balance sheet during this period.

The Major Investment Banks: Tangible Stockholders' Equity   Table VI.5

Source of underlying data: Company Annual Reports

		TSE as % of Total Adjusted Assets
1999		3.7%
2000		4.2%
2001		4.0%
2002		3.9%
2003	Acceleration	4.1%
2004	Phase	3.8%
2005		3.6%
2006	Deceleration	3.6%
Average		3.9%

Contrary to popular criticisms, the major investment banks did NOT increase leverage during the housing bubble — tangible stockholders' equity was relatively constant.

The analysis in Table VI.5 shows that the Street *did* operate with very high levels of leverage in the years leading up to the financial crisis, but also that this was essentially par for the period under study. Tangible stockholders' equity was 3.7% of tangible adjusted assets in 1999, rose slightly for a number of years, and then finished the period at 3.6%, about where it started out.

These are high levels of leverage, but they are levels that Wall Street was quite accustomed to functioning with. This undercuts the contemporary criticism that a lack of regulatory oversight enabled Wall Street to leverage up heedlessly during the bubble in a way that led to the crisis.

Liabilities

Now we'll see if anything unusual appears in the data on liabilities. I have bundled the investment banks' liabilities into three categories. Business liabilities are primarily payables and securities sold short, but I have also included deposits (which ranged from 2% to 6% and ended up at 4% of adjusted assets) to simplify the presentation. Collateralized financings consist primarily of securities sold under

The Major Investment Banks: Liabilities   **Table VI.6**

Source of underlying data: Company Annual Reports

		As a % of Adjusted Total Assets			
		Business Liabilities	Collateralized Finance Liabilities	Unsecured Borrowing Liabilities	Total Adjusted Liabilities
1999		43%	31%	22%	96%
2000		46%	30%	20%	96%
2001		48%	28%	20%	96%
2002		47%	29%	20%	96%
2003	Acceleration	47%	30%	19%	96%
2004	Phase	46%	31%	20%	96%
2005		42%	36%	19%	96%
2006	Deceleration	41%	35%	21%	96%
Average		45%	31%	20%	96%

The liability structure of the investment banks remained relatively constant during the housing bubble.

agreements to repurchase. Unsecured borrowings consist of both short-term and long-term borrowings.

Again, nothing jumps out as especially striking in the analysis of liabilities presented in Table VI.6, other than perhaps the rise in securitized financings from 31% of adjusted combined assets in 2004 to 36% in 2005.

Unsecured Borrowings

One criticism of Wall Street during this time was that it became increasingly dependent on what some referred to as "runnable" sources of finance, and the increase in collateralized financings may provide some indication of this. However, even here the evidence is somewhat less conclusive than we might have expected given the focus that some critics have put on this issue. This is especially true in the context of the following analysis.

In the previous table, I lumped all unsecured borrowings together. In Table VI.7 below, unsecured borrowings are divided into long-term and short-term obligations.

The Major Investment Banks: Unsecured Borrowings   **Table VI.7**

Source of underlying data: Company Annual Reports

		As a % of Adjusted Total Assets		
		Short-term Unsecured Borrowings	Long-term Unsecured Borrowings	Total Unsecured Borrowings
1999		10%	12%	22%
2000		6%	14%	20%
2001		6%	14%	20%
2002		7%	14%	20%
2003	Acceleration	5%	14%	19%
2004	Phase	4%	16%	20%
2005		4%	15%	19%
2006	Deceleration	4%	17%	21%
Average		6%	14%	20%

Total unsecured borrowings remained relatively constant during the housing bubble.

Given the idea that Wall Street was becoming overly dependent on "runnable" sources of finance, it is interesting to note that unsecured short-term borrowing actually *declined* from 10% of adjusted total assets in 1999 to 4% in 2006.

Exposure to Short-Term Financings

In order to understand the investment banks' *total* exposure to short-term financing obligations, it is necessary to group short-term *unsecured* borrowings with the short-term liabilities related to *secured* financings. Looking at combined short-term borrowings in this way yields the results shown in Table VI.8.

This analysis reveals that short-term financings were actually at a peak of 41% in 1999, then dropped to a low of 34% in 2001 and remained around this level before climbing back up to 39% in 2005 and 2006. All of which leads to the conclusion that reliance on short-term capital was at the high end of the range as the crisis approached, but not outside that range.

The Major Investment Banks: Short-Term Borrowings **Table VI.8**

Source of underlying data: Company Annual Reports

		Combined Secured & Unsecured Short-Term Borrowings as % of Total Adjusted Assets	
1999		41%	
2000		36%	
2001		34%	
2002		36%	*Some have asserted the investment banks became increasingly exposed to short-term "runnable" sources of finance during the bubble. In fact, however, total short-term borrowings were actually slightly lower in 2006 than they had been in 1999.*
2003	Acceleration	34%	
2004	Phase	35%	
2005		39%	
2006	Deceleration	39%	
Average		37%	

POSTMORTEM

The investment banks' assets grew at a relatively fast but *not* reckless pace of about 16% per year from 1999 through 2006. Trading and investment assets as a percentage of total assets increased somewhat in the early years of this period and then flattened out, primarily because mortgage and real estate assets increased from about 5% of total assets in 1999 to 11% in 2002 and then stabilized in the following years. Derivative positions started this period at about 7% of total assets, grew a bit for a few years thereafter, but then dropped off to 5.5% of total assets in 2006.

Contrary to contemporary criticism, tangible stockholders' equity as a percentage of total adjusted assets remained remarkably constant over the course of the period analyzed, starting at 3.7% in 1999 and ending at 3.6% in 2006. While these are indeed high levels of leverage, the analysis shows that Wall Street was used to operating with these levels of debt prior to the crisis.

On the liability side, unsecured short-term borrowings actually dropped from 10% of adjusted total assets in 1999 to 4% in 2006. Even if we add secured short-term borrowings to unsecured short-term borrowings, Wall Street's reliance on short-term capital did not change dramatically over this period.

The one development that pops out from this analysis is the increase in mortgage and real estate holdings, from 5% of adjusted total assets in 1999 to 11% in 2006. Given the magnitude of the mortgage finance boom that transpired during these years, however, I was somewhat surprised that the increase here was not even greater. The most obvious explanation for the relatively controlled increase in mortgage exposure is Wall Street's role as a packager and seller of mortgage securities, which served to limit the need to stockpile such assets.

Except for the rise in mortgages from 1999 to 2002 (which then stabilized during the Acceleration phase), Wall Street generally operated within consistent parameters through the years of the housing bubble. How then are we to account for the remarkable difficulties encountered by some of these institutions during the financial crisis?

While all five major investment banks experienced severe stress during the crisis, the financing markets ascertained key differences in the risk profiles of the individual investment banks. Even in the midst of the Panic stage, some of the investment banks were able to access privately placed capital, whereas others were not able to do so. Hence, we can use the differing assessments of the capital markets at the time to help identify the critical measure of financial strength or weakness that distinguished the investment banks that were able to access private capital from those that were not. The five investment banks can be sorted into three categories:

The Most-Endangered Investment Banks

In March 2008, Bear Stearns began to experience capital runs that put the firm's survival in jeopardy. For the first time in history, the Federal Reserve decided to provide bailout financing to save an investment bank; such financing helped induce J.P. Morgan to acquire Bear Stearns. The Fed's bailout and the distressed sale to J.P. Morgan make it clear that Bear belongs in the "most endangered" category of major investment banks.

Lehman Brothers' bankruptcy in September 2008 tells us that Lehman also belongs in this category.

The Middle Tier

Like Lehman, Merrill Lynch began to experience severe financing difficulties as 2008 wore on. In part because of the perceived value of its vast and highly respected retail brokerage operation, however, Merrill was able to enter into a contract for the distressed sale of itself to Bank of America. When the sale to BofA was originally announced, there was no federal bailout financing involved, though this would later change when Merrill's mortgage portfolio deteriorated severely in the fourth quarter of the year.

The fact that Merrill was forced into a distressed sale tells us that it was undergoing financing pressures similar to those experienced by Bear and Lehman. At the same time, Merrill's ability to arrange a sale that initially did not require government assistance tells us that Merrill was in a safer place than its failed counterparts.

The Least-Endangered Investment Banks

The Panic stage of the financial crisis started when Lehman was unexpectedly allowed to fail on September 15, 2008. At roughly the same time that Lehman's bankruptcy was announced, Merrill announced its sale to Bank of America, which temporarily helped put Merrill in a safe place. These developments, plus the earlier sale of Bear Stearns to J.P. Morgan, left Morgan Stanley and Goldman Sachs exposed to the vicissitudes of a panicking financial market.

In spite of the extreme difficulty of these circumstances, first Goldman and then Morgan were able to arrange private market financings that helped assure the capital markets that these firms were capable of surviving the turmoil. Goldman Sachs announced a private placement of $5 billion of preferred stock to Warren Buffett's Berkshire Hathaway on September 23, and Morgan Stanley announced a $9 billion private placement to Mitsubishi, the Japanese financial consortium, on October 13.

These private financings tell us that Goldman and Morgan were the *least* endangered of the five major investment banks in the eyes of the financial markets at the time.

The Critical Measure

An explanation of exactly what scared the financial markets about the investment banks during the Panic stage must account for these differing outcomes. I believe the best way to understand how the markets likely weighed the risks of the major investment banks is to look at tangible stockholders' equity (TSE) as a percentage of mortgages and other real estate assets for each firm. If we assume that other assets were at least worth book value, then TSE as a percentage of the book value of mortgages and real estate assets provides a measure of how far these endangered asset values could fall before a firm became insolvent. At a relatively safe firm, TSE as a percentage of mortgage and real estate assets would be expected to be higher than at a less secure firm.

Table VI.9 shows TSE as a percentage of mortgage and real estate assets as of the 2007 fiscal year's end for each of the five investment banks. Lehman, Bear, and Merrill were in similar positions heading into 2008, with TSE ranging from 18% to 26% of mortgages and real estate assets. The key distinguishing factor among the three was Merrill's retail brokerage operation, which gave the firm a very high level of economic value that was not reflected in the book value of

The Major Investment Banks: Tangible Stockholders' Equity as a Percentage of Mortgage & Real Estate Assets   **Table VI.9**

Source of underlying data: Company Annual Reports

Most Endangered	Fiscal Year End 2007 TSE*	
Lehman Brothers	18%	*Lehman and Bear had the lowest levels of TSE* relative to mortgages & RE, and thus were most at risk when the collapse of the bubble threatened these asset values.*
Bear Stearns	24%	
Merrill Lynch	26%	*Merrill was similarly capitalized, but the intangible value of its retail brokerage business made it an attractive acquisition target.*
Least Endangered		
Goldman Sachs	70%	*Goldman and Morgan were highly capitalized relative to mortgage & RE exposure, which helped insulate them from a fall in mortgage values. Both were able to raise private capital and ride out the crisis.*
Morgan Stanley	84%	

* TSE = Tangible Stockholders' Equity

its assets. Lacking this type of "non-book" economic value, Lehman and Bear were highly exposed. A drop of just 18% to 24% in the value of their mortgage and real estate holdings—assuming the liquidation value of all other assets was equal to book value—would have rendered each insolvent.

On the other hand, Morgan Stanley and Goldman were quite well positioned to withstand even the most severe housing downturn. At Goldman, it would have taken roughly a 70% decline in the value of the firm's mortgage positions to wipe out TSE, whereas Morgan Stanley was protected up to a drop of 84%.

Looking at the firms in this way, and taking the non-book economic value of Merrill's retail operations into consideration, it is quite understandable that: (1) Bear and Lehman failed, (2) Merrill was initially able to arrange a distressed sale of itself that did *not* require bailout financing, and (3) Goldman and Morgan were able to access private sources of capital that allowed them to survive as standalone companies.

SUMMARY

When accounting problems and the Fed's interest rate policies pushed the GSEs out of the driver's seat of the bubble, the major investment banks, along with large commercial banks like Citigroup, stepped in to fill the gap, primarily through mortgage securitizations. Even though the investment banks were not generally in the business of holding mortgage assets on their books, they did need to hold some such assets to support their securitization efforts.

Collectively, mortgage and other real estate assets grew from 5% of total assets in 1999 to 11% in 2006. This increase was not particularly alarming on its own, but it did cause the ratio of tangible stockholders' equity to mortgage and related assets to decline over time, which left Bear and Lehman in especially vulnerable positions as the crisis unfolded. While similarly exposed, Merrill was in a better position than Bear and Lehman because of its highly valued retail brokerage operation and was therefore able to negotiate a distressed sale to Bank of America. Finally, Goldman and Morgan were well positioned to weather the storm, which is likely why they were able to access private funding that helped them survive as standalone entities.

–30–

MONEY MARKET MUTUAL FUNDS

Let's now turn our attention to the role the money market mutual funds played in the crisis.

At the outset, it should be noted that the mutual fund industry did not cause the crisis nor did it significantly worsen things, but it did have the potential to make the crisis much worse than it actually was. More severe problems were avoided only because a number of money market mutual funds were bailed out. Initially, fund sponsors seeking to protect their business reputations funded the bailouts. Then, when problems emerged at a fund whose sponsor was incapable of executing such a bailout, the government authorities adeptly stepped in to backstop the entire industry. If not for these bailouts, money market mutual funds would have experienced more severe runs on their assets. These runs would have forced such funds to sell commercial paper and other short-term financial instruments into a panicking market, which would have exacerbated the crisis.

Recognizing these risks might seem to support the narrative that the financial system would somehow have been better off if more of its business had been conducted through the more heavily regulated banking system. But this misses three key points.

First, as we have seen, even the more heavily regulated parts of the system such as the GSEs and Citigroup experienced the same problems that the less regulated parts did.

Second, the authorities did not understand what was happening as the housing bubble swelled to such dangerous proportions. This was true of the congressional overseers of the GSEs, whose housing policies aided and abetted the expansion that triggered the Liftoff phase of the bubble, and it was true of the officials at the Fed, who did not understand how their interest rate policies fueled the Acceleration phase.

Third, the notion that the problems with the mutual funds may have evidenced a greater need for regulation misses the point that earlier problems with the banking regulatory system actually gave rise to the money market mutual fund industry in the first place.

Nevertheless, the problems that the money market fund industry faced during the financial crisis were magnified by and did help expose what I will call the industry's "Original Sin," an accounting fiction that both the fund industry and the regulatory system bear responsibility for. This Original Sin received a great deal of well-deserved attention in the aftermath of the crisis. Unfortunately, while the authorities did focus on the right issues and courageously stood up to the industry to enact some improvements, I believe that the ultimate changes did not go far enough.

The discussion that follows briefly summarizes how the money market mutual fund industry arose out of failures in the banking regulatory model, the mutual fund industry's Original Sin, how it played into the financial crisis, and how—in the aftermath of the crisis—only a suboptimal regulatory solution was achieved.

FROM FAILED BANKING REGULATIONS TO MONEY MARKET MUTUAL FUNDS

The modern system of banking regulation was established during the Great Depression. In the relatively benign post–World War II economy, this system worked reasonably well for a while. By the late 1960s, however, it started to show an inability to adapt to changing times. This caused a number of problems, one of which led to the creation of the money market mutual fund industry.

Let's begin by going back to the 1930s and the origin of the banking regulatory system amidst the confusion of the Great Depression.

We now know that the Depression was caused by a combination of the collapse of the European monetary system under the weight of the unsustainable government borrowings and inflations undertaken to finance World War I, and the failed policies of the Federal Reserve. Unfortunately, decades passed before all of this was understood.

The mistaken idea that the Depression was caused by private market failure arose in part because the banking failures that plagued the nation in the early 1930s brought the collapse of the international and domestic monetary systems very close to nearly everyone's home. Iconic black-and-white photos of forlorn people in drab overcoats standing in seemingly endless bank lines with the hope of withdrawing some of their life savings helped sear the failure of the banking system into the nation's consciousness. I still remember visiting my grandparents in the tiny farm town of Tipton, Iowa, as a young child and listening as one of my older cousins, working on a school assignment, interviewed my grandpa about what it was like to live through the Depression. He responded that the first thing that came to mind was the long lines of scared people hoping to get their money out of the local bank for fear that it might fail.

As Milton Friedman later pointed out, this situation could have been avoided, but "the Federal Reserve had failed to do what it was originally set up to do. It had permitted a collapse of the monetary system, it had permitted perfectly sound banks to fail by the thousands because of liquidity problems, although it had been set up in 1913 with the objective of preventing that kind of situation."[1]

In the midst of the Fed's misguided policy response and the confusion about the real causes of the Depression, Franklin Roosevelt and his advisers created a program of government-backed deposit insurance. The premise was that government insurance would reassure depositors that their funds were safe, thereby mitigating the risk that bank runs like those witnessed by my grandfather would exacerbate future panics. This system was initially supported even by free-market-oriented economists like Friedman, who argued that "since the Fed had failed and showed no sign that it was not going to continue to fail in pursuing its function, something else was needed to perform the function for which it had originally been established and that the Federal Deposit Insurance Corporation would serve that function."[2]

While the deposit insurance system did seem to work pretty much as designed in the decades immediately following its creation, it must be recognized that the economically robust post–World War II years did not present much of a test. By the 1960s, however, the banking regulatory model erected alongside the deposit insurance system began to exhibit a problem not uncommon to such schemes: an inability to adapt to changing times and circumstances, followed by subsequent "fixes" that then lead to new problems of their own.

In the discussion of the origin and growth of the GSEs (Fannie Mae and Freddie Mac), we saw that one problem with the financial regulatory system had to do with its inability to provide capital to the areas that needed it most. Specifically, the regulatory model for banks and for savings and loans tended to keep deposits locked up in slower-growth areas like the Northeast and the Midwest. As the nation grew and migrated over time, however, high-growth regions like California and Florida were faced with a shortage of funds for housing. Unfortunately, given the heavy federal spending on the Vietnam War and the Great Society programs, the "solution" to this regional funding problem was the creation of the modern government-sponsored enterprises. We have already seen how that worked out.

Around the time the modern GSEs were established, further problems arose with the financial regulatory model, and once again we find misguided Federal Reserve policies at the heart of the matter. As Milton Friedman and Anna Schwartz demonstrated, the Fed's mistake during the 1930s was failing to provide the financial system with liquidity when it needed it most. Amidst the guns-and-butter spending of the late 1960s and early '70s, the Fed made the opposite mistake: in an ill-fated attempt to help the federal government fund the Vietnam War and the Great Society programs without raising taxes or adding to the federal debt, the Fed expanded the money supply too rapidly. This excess money creation led to the so-called stagflation (high inflation combined with high unemployment and anemic growth) that plagued the 1970s.

Rising rates of inflation pushed up interest rates, which in turn caused the value of long-term fixed-income investments—like the thirty-year fixed-rate mortgages held on the books of the S&L system—to fall. The declining value of its portfolio of mortgages effectively bankrupted the S&L industry. This problem only worsened in the 1980s when the Reagan administration attempted to resolve these issues through ill-conceived deregulation that allowed S&L executives to go on a reckless expansion funded by taxpayer-backed deposits. By the 1990s, the S&L industry that had long played an important role in housing finance was essentially dead on arrival. As a consequence, more of the housing finance system migrated to the GSEs, and later to the less regulated parts of the "shadow banking system."

In addition to bankrupting the S&Ls, the high interest rates resulting from the Fed's inflation also exposed problems in the banking side of the regulatory system. One important element of this system, known as Regulation Q, imposed strict ceilings on the interest rates that banks could pay depositors. As inflation pushed market rates of interest above the Reg Q ceilings, however, investors were faced with a loss of purchasing power if they left their savings in the banking system. The money market mutual fund industry arose as a solution to these regulatory problems.

THE ORIGINS OF MONEY MARKET MUTUAL FUNDS

The first money market mutual fund (MMF) was created in 1972. As Professor Jonathan Macey of Yale observed, "MMFs experienced their initial period of rapid growth in 1974 and 1975, as a result of Regulation Q's strict ceiling on the interest rates that insured depository institutions were permitted to pay."[3]

During the mid-1970s, the maximum interest rate that Reg Q allowed banks to pay depositors hovered around 5%. The high rates of inflation resulting from unrestrained government spending and the Fed's policies, however, caused market rates of interest to rise well above the Reg Q ceilings during certain periods. Rates on three-month Treasury bills rose as high as 7–8% in the early 1970s and then spiked up to well above 10% in the late '70s and early '80s.

Because of Reg Q, investors who had their money tied up in the banking system saw the purchasing power of their savings eroded by the Fed's inflation, the consequences of which fell especially hard on those who had few saving alternatives. As the Fed itself later acknowledged, "Deposit interest rate ceilings discriminated against the relatively less wealthy savers. When market interest rates were above ceiling rates, the wealthier investors shifted their deposits to money market securities."[4]

Much as the first equity mutual funds had democratized access to investing in diversified pools of common stocks, the money market mutual fund industry democratized access to the ownership of Treasury bills, commercial paper, and other forms of short-term interest-paying securities. Further, the overall benefits of such funds made them a better vehicle for wealthier investors as well.

As a result, the industry flourished and became an important and highly efficient source of short-term financing in the U.S. capital markets. As Marcin Kacperczyk and Philipp Schnabl of NYU noted with respect to such funds, "They are the largest provider of short-term financing in the U.S. economy, similar in size to the entire sector of equity mutual funds, and they are the largest provider of liquidity to U.S. corporations, issuing about the same amount of demand deposits as the entire U.S. commercial banking sector."[5]

Unlike the GSEs, the money market mutual fund industry was an extraordinarily successful response to the failures that emerged in the financial regulatory system. Nevertheless, as the financial crisis revealed, the money fund industry owes some measure of its success to what I call its Original Sin.

ORIGINAL SIN

The creators of the first money market mutual funds knew that investors in such funds were concerned about more than just higher yields. Because these new vehicles were parking places for cash, they also needed to be perceived as safe and stable—in other words, if investors were going to put their short-term savings in a money market mutual fund instead of a bank, they would want to feel comfortable that their principal investment would remain intact and could be withdrawn at any time. Furthermore, some potential money market fund investors, such as trust departments, were *required* to hold cash in stable value securities. As Matthew Fink, former president of the Investment Company Institute, noted, "Trustees could not put their clients' money in any investment that had a fluctuating net asset value, no matter how high the returns might be, for fear of losing money through a sudden market change."[6]

The industry took a number of sensible steps to achieve these objectives, such as investing in diversified pools of high-quality, short-term money market instruments, but potential issues remained: (1) a sudden rise in interest rates could still cause a fund's net asset value (NAV) to decline, or (2) a default by the issuer of the securities held by a fund could cause its NAV to drop, or (3) both of these things could happen. Any such losses might be small and relatively contained, but they were virtually unavoidable over time.

One approach to dealing with these realities would have been for the fund industry to acknowledge them and take the responsibility of educating investors as to why the risk of a slight loss in value could be worth taking. The pitch for the newly minted money market mutual funds could have been something along the lines of: "There is a small chance that, in some rare circumstances, an investor may get slightly less than her original investment back when she redeems her interest in the fund, but because we believe that such risks are low and because the fund is currently earning returns that are so much higher than those available in a bank savings account, we think this risk is well worth it. In addition, there is also the potential for investors to get back slightly *more* than they invested under certain circumstances, like a decline in interest rates." This is basically a version of the pitch that the investment community learned to make as it persuaded savers to pull long-term funds out of banks and fixed-income investments and put them in stocks—a pitch that has served investors, the industry, and the economy quite well.

For those savers who needed to ensure maximum stability for their short-term investments, the money fund industry could have developed products that owned securities of only the very highest credit ratings with extremely short-term maturities. True, such funds would have had lower yields than many of the money fund products actually offered, but this would have forced investors to select the tradeoff between yield and stability that best fit their needs.

The issue with these alternative approaches, however, is that they would have made the newly created money funds less easily marketable. So the industry chose instead to pursue an accounting fiction that made the money market mutual funds *appear* to be much more like the familiar savings deposits that the funds were attracting money away from. Rather than reporting actual—fluctuating—net asset values (NAVs) and redeeming shares at actual NAV (which in some cases would have been slightly above or below the $1.00 share price that became the money market fund standard), the industry chose accounting methods that created the *illusion* of a stable $1.00 share value. This reporting made it appear that such funds provided the safety of a bank account together with the higher yields of money market instruments.

In practice, this approach was not a *big* lie, since deviations in value from the fictitious $1.00 tended to be very small. But it did contribute to the idea that *all* money market mutual funds were essentially the same and that one could always expect to redeem one's investment at original cost, much as would be the case with a bank savings account.

This was unfortunate, as was the decision by the regulatory community to condone such practices. Over time, and even after public hearings, the SEC effectively sanctioned these practices subject to certain regulatory limitations, which were eventually codified under rule 2a-7 of the Investment Company Act.

To be clear, industry conduct within the confines of the regulatory standards worked exceptionally well. But the fact remained that the money market mutual fund industry chose to operate under an accounting fiction that misrepresented the reality of their products, and the regulatory authorities sanctioned this misrepresentation. While this wasn't much of an issue in normal times, the financial crisis was no normal time.

BREAKING THE BUCK

From the time of its founding in the early 1970s, the money market mutual fund industry has been extraordinarily successful because it serves an important need for more efficient and adaptable cash management than the regulated banking system could provide, and because it has been well managed and guided by generally sound but not excessive regulation. There were a handful of incidents in the late 1980s and early '90s when such funds suffered losses that would have caused them to "break the buck" and return less than the full amount of investor principal; but in each of those cases, fund sponsors, seeking to protect their business reputations, stepped in to bail out the tarnished funds. In the mid-'90s, one small fund catering to community banks incurred losses that led to a liquidation of the fund for less than $1.00 per share. This was the first and only time that such a fund was forced to "break the buck"—until the Financial Crisis of 2008.[7]

As noted in the October 2010 Report of the President's Working Group on Financial Markets, "Beginning in mid-2007, dozens of funds faced losses from holdings of highly rated asset-backed commercial paper (ABCP) issued by structured investment vehicles (SIVs), some of which had exposures to the subprime mortgage market."[8]

A key development in the decade leading up to the crisis was the popularity of money market mutual funds catering to large institutional investors. Known as institutional money market funds, they often required an initial minimum investment of $1 million. By 2008, assets in these funds were almost double the assets held in funds targeted to smaller retail investors.

One large institutional fund, the Prime Reserve Fund, had a little over 1% of its assets invested in Lehman Brothers paper when Lehman filed bankruptcy. The Prime Fund's sponsor did not have the resources to bail it out, which forced the fund to reduce redemption prices to $0.97 per share. This "breaking of the buck" by a large money market fund led to the beginnings of a run that then spread to similar funds. According to the President's Working Group report, during the week that Lehman filed for bankruptcy, investors sought to withdraw funds representing roughly 15% of the holdings of prime institutional funds. This run on prime money market mutual funds was the modern-day equivalent of the Depression-era bank runs witnessed by my grandfather.

In large part because of Friedman and Schwartz's work, this time the authorities did not make the same mistakes in dealing with the MMFs that were made with respect to the larger banking system during the Depression. To stem the run on money market funds, the authorities adroitly stepped in to establish a well-structured temporary guarantee fund to backstop money market fund losses. Fund outflows slowed immediately, and by mid-October, money market funds were again attracting net inflows.

As I showed earlier, key measures of overall financial market stress remained at high levels even as the run on the money funds abated. Furthermore, these highly stressed conditions in the general markets persisted until the last of the critical financial institutions was bailed out in early 2009. This tells us that the money market fund industry did not cause the financial crisis and that the backstops provided by the Fed and Treasury did not end the crisis. Nevertheless, the authorities clearly took important steps here that helped keep the crisis from spinning further out of control.

Also, for the first time since the dawn of the money fund industry, the potential risks resulting from its Original Sin were exposed in a way that was not to be ignored.

REGULATORY RESPONSE

In the immediate aftermath of the financial crisis, the SEC added new rules and regulations designed to further reduce the risk of runs on money market mutual funds. The President's Working Group report released in 2010 set forth additional policy options for consideration, one of which included the establishment of a two-tier system wherein institutional money market mutual funds would report and redeem shares based on a floating net asset value (NAV), while retail funds would continue to operate with the stable value, $1.00 per share, reporting convention. In 2014, the SEC announced that it would adopt this two-tiered model along with other provisions.

Many in the fund industry strongly opposed these changes, and the authorities deserve credit for making the switch to a floating NAV model for institutional funds. But I believe the changes made were less than ideal and should have gone even further. Specifically, in converting the institutional fund market to floating NAV, the SEC carved out an exception for government money market funds, which were allowed to maintain $1.00-per-share stable value reporting. Not surprisingly, this resulted in a wholesale shift out of prime institutional funds and into government funds. While funds holding government securities are less likely to experience runs, the use of stable value reporting is still based on the fiction that government funds won't fluctuate in value, when in fact such funds will still be at risk of fluctuations due to interest rate changes.

Additionally, stable value reporting for government funds may conceal other risks that could develop over time. True, the risk of direct losses in funds holding federal government paper is diminished by the ability of the government to print money to fund its debts and obligations. But this only obscures the potential decline in creditworthiness that occurs if a government borrows and prints money indiscriminately, as was the case when Europe's unsustainable debts and inflations caused the collapse of the international monetary system during the Great Depression.

As the stagflation of the 1970s showed, such risks are not unique to foreign governments. High inflation is essentially a de facto default. Permitting government money market funds to continue operating under the Original Sin of stable value reporting diminishes the incentives for investors to take such risks into consideration, which increases the potential for inefficient discrimination between government and nongovernment debt. All of this can lead to inefficient capital allocation *and* reduced incentives for government to operate and finance itself in a disciplined manner. Events in the twentieth century show that this is not merely a theoretical matter.

Instead of carving out government funds for special treatment, a far better solution would have been to put all institutional funds, both government and prime, on a level playing field in accounting, reporting, and redeeming; and then to require all such funds to report the percentage of redemptions that are made within various ranges around the objective of staying as close as possible to a real stable value per share. Such data would enable investors to make meaningful and realistic evaluations of the benefits of money market funds versus other options for parking short-term cash.

Some have argued that this is not a viable solution because many institutional charters prohibit investing in funds with a variable NAV. But such funds are already investing in variable NAV vehicles, which are just not reporting the reality of what happens in the funds. If the benefits of variable NAV funds are better than the alternatives, change the charter; but don't maintain a pretense that is inconsistent with reality.

I believe it was also a mistake to leave the Original Sin of stable value reporting in place for retail money market funds. No matter how strict the regulations, such reporting obscures the underlying realities of these funds, which increases the risk that they will be misunderstood by investors. Furthermore, any increase in size and importance resulting from such fictions will lead to inefficient capital allocation and increase the risks of substantial unexpected losses and runs in future crises.

While many in the fund industry do not see things this way, I believe that these changes, over time, would be in their own best interest. The history of the banking regulatory scheme recounted above and the shorter history of the money fund industry both indicate that staying the present path will likely lead to increasingly complex and restrictive layers of regulation. This is likely to hobble the fund industry with the same inability to adapt to change that doomed the banking system and gave rise to money market mutual funds in the first place.

While it may not seem obvious now, the industry would be better served by moving to accounting, reporting, and redeeming shares on a basis that reflects the underlying realities within their funds and then explaining the benefits of these funds to investors vis-à-vis their alternatives. This is basically how the equity mutual fund industry grew to be such a durable and dominant part of the investment landscape.

SUMMARY

The money market mutual fund industry arose because of the inability of the banking regulatory system to evolve to meet the nation's changing financial needs. In particular, the Fed's runaway inflation during the 1970s pushed market interest rates above the levels that banks were allowed to pay under Regulation Q, thereby diminishing the purchasing power of funds deposited in the banking system. On the whole, the money market fund industry was a well-conceived and well-executed market response to these problems, and in general the fund industry operated exceptionally well in the ensuing decades.

In order to attract more money more quickly, however, the money fund industry committed the Original Sin of adopting stable value reporting, which masked the fluctuating asset values of their products, created the unreasonable expectation that all investors would be able to withdraw their investments at par under all circumstances, and failed to provide a reason for investors to discriminate between the investment practices of different money market funds. The regulatory authorities then sanctioned these misguided practices.

The financial crisis exposed the problems in the fund industry's structure. The Fed and other authorities, having learned from mistakes made during the Great Depression, implemented liquidity supports that helped keep the MMF industry from exacerbating the financial crisis. In the aftermath, a new regulatory regime arose that made some improvements to industry reporting, especially with respect to prime institutional funds. Unfortunately, however, the new regulations allowed stable value reporting to continue for both government institutional funds and retail funds.

ALTERNATIVE THEORIES OF THE CRISIS

One alternative theory of the crisis is that it was somehow caused by deregulation. Another is that a supposed global savings glut led to the unprecedented escalation of housing prices. It's also possible that fundamental factors such as building costs or home affordability played an important role in the housing bubble. Let's examine each of these theories.

THE DEREGULATION NARRATIVE

Perhaps the most widely held view of the crisis is that it was caused by deregulation. As recently as July 2020, a Google search for "What caused the financial crisis of 2008" elicited this leading answer: "The financial crisis was primarily caused by deregulation of the financial industry."

In the immediate aftermath of the crisis, much of the blame was focused on Wall Street investment banks, which represented the least heavily regulated sector of the financial markets. Furthermore, the event that first provoked a broad-based public reaction was the Fed's historic decision to provide bailout financing to facilitate J.P. Morgan's purchase of Bear Stearns. This was the first time the Fed had ever bailed out an investment bank, and the decision evoked bipartisan howls of protest from those who saw it as a bailout of Wall Street fat cats, from those who disliked the idea of federal intervention in the markets, and from others who saw it as evidence that Wall Street was playing a rigged game of "heads I win, tails you lose." In other words, almost everyone (other than, perhaps, Bear Stearns and J.P. Morgan) hated the bailout.

If the Bear Stearns bailout didn't get everyone's attention, the failure of Lehman Brothers certainly did. Lehman's failure led to a precipitous drop in the stock market, to political turmoil as federal authorities and Congress groped to quell the unrest, to the freezing up of capital markets in a manner that affected everything from home loans to consumer finance, and to a recession that put many people out of work. Indeed, during the 2008 presidential debate in the midst of the post-Lehman chaos, the candidates from both major parties fingered underregulated Wall Street greed as the cause of the crisis. Later on, the highly publicized Occupy Wall Street protests branded the idea of Wall Street's culpability onto the nation's consciousness, as did a stream of best-selling books and Hollywood productions portraying unchecked Wall Street greed as a primary culprit in the financial crisis.

Some factors did *seem* to support the idea that lax regulation was the underlying cause of the crisis. As noted, Wall Street investment banks were the least regulated of the critical financial institutions in the eye of the storm. Furthermore, surging demand for adjustable-rate mortgages in the 2000s led to a vast expansion of mortgage securitizations, which Wall Street was only too happy to accommodate. Hence, the bubble was the first housing cycle in which Wall Street securitizations played a major role.

Nevertheless, the idea that deregulation caused the crisis was initially little more than a popular narrative in search of a supporting theory. As we saw with respect to both the 1830s, when Andrew Jackson closed the Second Bank of the United States, and the Great

Depression of the 1930s, narratives that seem compelling can lead to highly misleading conclusions about even the most consequential events. Once firmly established in the national consciousness, those misleading conclusions can persist for generations and lead to inappropriate policies—policies that actually cause future crises.

The more rigorous proponents of the deregulation narrative realized the need for a testable theory of how deregulation could have led to the Financial Crisis of 2008. Not surprisingly, they focused on the idea that the allegedly underregulated investment banks caused the crisis. As we saw above, some widely accepted allegations regarding the investment banks were repeated so frequently that almost everyone assumed them to be true—until someone bothered to check the facts.

Some observers posited that Wall Street was able to leverage itself up dangerously in a reckless pursuit of profit because of a relaxation of SEC rules governing investment banks. This was factually incorrect in two ways. Consistent with the analysis of the investment banks presented earlier, a report prepared for the *Journal of Economic Literature* found "much higher levels of leverage in 1998 than 2006 for Goldman Sachs, Merrill Lynch, and Lehman Brothers. Moreover, it turns out that the SEC rule change had no effect on leverage restrictions."[1]

Another problem with the idea that allegedly underregulated investment banks caused the crisis is that the investment banks weren't the only critical financial institutions that reached the point of failure. If either of the GSEs (Fannie Mae or Freddie Mac) or the critical commercial banks (Citigroup or Bank of America) had been treated the way that Lehman was, the resulting failure would have produced the same result that Lehman's failure did—as evidenced by the panic-level readings in both the S&P 500 and the TED spread that persisted until *all* of these critical institutions had been bailed out. It makes no sense, then, to single out the investment banks when the highly regulated GSEs and commercial banks were just as dependent on bailout financing as Bear Stearns and Lehman Brothers and just as capable of provoking a panic.

Perhaps the most plausible support for the deregulation theory was the oft-repeated assertion that the crisis resulted from the repeal of Glass-Steagall, formally called the Banking Act of 1933, which had separated commercial banking from investment banking. After all, the Graham-Leach-Bliley Act (GLB), which ended Glass-Steagall, was signed into law in 1999, just as the bubble started to expand.

The problem with this version of the deregulation argument is that GLB didn't make any changes that affected the course of events. The GSEs and the investment banks had always been free to underwrite and hold mortgage securities, so the repeal of Glass-Steagall did *not* affect their role in the housing bubble. Further, the Federal Reserve itself had cleared commercial banks to underwrite mortgage securities as far back as 1986, so GLB did not make any substantive changes that affected their role during the bubble.

Barry Eichengreen of UC Berkeley, even as he restated the general deregulation argument, acknowledged that GLB played no role in the financial crisis:

> It would be all too easy to claim that Glass-Steagall's death was a singular event that caused the financial crisis. In fact, its demise was the culmination of a decades-long process of financial deregulation in which both commercial banks and shadow banks were permitted to engage in a wider range of activities, while supervision and oversight lagged behind. Competition between commercial banks, investment banks, and shadow banks squeezed the profits of all involved. Many of the affected institutions responded by using more borrowed money and assuming more risk. The consequences, we know, were disastrous.[2]

Here, Mr. Eichengreen has stated the deregulation argument as persuasively as possible; nevertheless, he has also returned the allegation to its original anecdotal form. It still lacks a testable hypothesis of how deregulation led to changes that could have unleashed such a historic chain of events.

A persuasive theory of the financial crisis must provide compelling explanations of why:

1. Housing markets that had functioned so well for so long suddenly began to inflate dramatically in 1998, and then exhibited such discrete turning points thereafter.
2. After a century of investment banking failures, none of which had provoked a financial panic, Lehman's failure set off the panic of 2008.

The gradual-deregulation theory does not explain these events.

There are other important questions that the deregulation argument fails to answer. If the problem was inadequate regulation and policy involvement, why did the highly regulated GSEs and Citigroup, which was overseen directly by the Federal Reserve and was perhaps the most high-profile commercial bank in the country, end up needing multiple rounds of bailout financing to survive? It would be hard to find three more prominent, publicly scrutinized and highly regulated financial institutions than Fannie Mae, Freddie Mac, and Citigroup—all of which would have ended up in the same place as Lehman Brothers but for the massive bailouts they received.

And if more regulation is the solution, why didn't the regulators and other authorities spot the dangers of the housing bubble? We know that the primary overseers in Congress, at OFHEO, and at the Federal Reserve were unaware of the looming crisis because their own policies actually caused the bubble. Then, as the bubble expanded and in its aftermath, key officials at the Fed not only denied responsibility but insisted on an alternative theory to explain what was happening with housing prices: the so-called "global savings glut" theory.

THE "GLOBAL SAVINGS GLUT"

Alan Greenspan was chairman of the Fed as the bubble expanded and Ben Bernanke was vice chairman before succeeding Greenspan in 2006. Both men floated the hypothesis of a "global savings glut" in response to charges that the Fed's interest rate policies were pushing up housing prices. According to this theory, which was first set forward in the mid-2000s, international capital flowing from developing countries like China into the United States pushed down long-term mortgage rates and fueled housing price appreciation.

In 2011, however, Bernanke and others at the Fed published an extensive report acknowledging that any role played by a global savings glut was of secondary importance to domestic causes of the housing bubble. In other words, the Fed's own analysis discredited the theory that an alleged global savings glut played an important role in the bubble.

If the leading bureaucrats did not understand the consequences of their own policies, how could we expect them to oversee a regulatory apparatus that would circumvent those consequences?

BUILDING COSTS

In addition to an index of real (inflation-adjusted) housing prices, Robert Shiller constructed an index of real building costs. To determine whether building costs played a role in the housing bubble, let's begin by comparing the relationship between real (inflation-adjusted) building costs and real housing prices over the years leading up to the bubble. Then we'll look at the relationship between building costs and housing prices during the Liftoff and the Acceleration.

During the fifteen years ending in 1997, real building costs *declined* at a compound rate of 0.8% per year. Over the same time, real housing prices *grew* at a compound rate of 0.3% per year.

In the four-year Base Period from 1994 through 1997, real building costs *increased* at a compound rate of 0.2% per year, while real housing prices *declined* by 0.2% per year.

Hence, in both the longer and the shorter period leading up to the Liftoff, there was little correlation between real building costs and real housing prices. Indeed, they moved in opposite directions during both those periods.

A similar pattern can be seen in the Liftoff phase of the bubble (1998–2001), when real building costs *declined* by 0.9% per year, but real housing prices *grew* by 4.7% per year. Changes in building costs therefore do not explain the sudden spike in housing prices at that time.

During Acceleration (2002–2005), the trends in the real housing price index and the building cost index did move in the same direction, though at nowhere near the same rate. Real building costs increased by an aggregate of 8%, while real housing prices increased by an aggregate of 38%, nearly five times as fast.

While there is almost certainly a connection between building costs and home price appreciation over long periods of time, changes in building costs do not explain the historic movements in housing prices that occurred during either the Liftoff or the Acceleration phase of the housing bubble.

HOME AFFORDABILITY

The National Association of Realtors (NAR) maintains a home affordability index that is a function of the NAR's national data on the median price for a single-family home, the Census Bureau's calculation of median family income, and the prevailing mortgage rate reported by the Federal Housing Finance Board. An index of 100 means that a family with the median income has exactly enough income to purchase a median-priced home.

As conventional mortgage rates dropped from around 15% in 1982 to 10% in 1989, the NAR's affordability index rose by an aggregate of 56%, which roughly matched the 54% increase in nominal home prices during this period. Declining interest rates then helped fuel further increases in home affordability until the mid-1990s, when mortgage rates stabilized at around 7.5%. During the four-year Base Period (1994–1997), home affordability dropped slightly (by 3%), as did real home prices (by an aggregate of 1%).

During the Liftoff phase of the bubble (1998–2001), however, affordability *increased* slightly (by 2%), even as real home prices surged upward by an aggregate of 20%. The relationship between affordability and home prices diverged further during the Acceleration phase, when the affordability index *declined* 12% while the real home price index *increased* by an aggregate of 38%. Needless to say, changes in home affordability do not explain the housing bubble.

SUMMARY

Neither building costs nor changes in home affordability drove the housing bubble. As the Fed's own analysis showed, the so-called global savings glut hypothesized by its former chairmen played, at most, a secondary role. The still widely accepted deregulation argument remains an anecdotally based narrative that (1) lacks a testable theory to support it, (2) is inconsistent with the data presented herein, and (3) posits a solution that is inconsistent with the failures of even the most highly regulated financial institutions and with the failure of the regulators themselves to understand what caused the housing bubble and the financial crisis.

PART VII

CONCLUSION

-32-

RECAP

The U.S. housing markets had operated for over a hundred years without experiencing anything even close to the national boom and bust that characterized the housing bubble. Indeed, the belief that this historic resilience would continue was a big reason that so many participants missed the danger when, beginning in the late 1990s, things suddenly changed in a dramatic and unprecedented way.

Likewise, the prior history of the inherently high-risk investment banking industry was littered with one failure after another, including Kidder Peabody, Salomon Brothers, Drexel Burnham, and EF Hutton, to name just a few in the decades preceding the financial crisis. But none of these prior failures had led to anything like the panic that accompanied the failure of Lehman Brothers in 2008.

What suddenly changed in the late 1990s and early 2000s that was capable of pushing the national housing market so far off the norms that had persisted for over a century? Why did Lehman's failure in 2008 provoke a panic when so many previous investment banking failures did not?

I believe that the theory set forth herein and summarized below answers these crucial questions.

BEFORE THE HOUSING BUBBLE

Long-Term Housing Prices (1890–1997): Robert Shiller's index of real (inflation-adjusted) housing prices shows that they grew by about 0.1% per year over inflation from 1890 to 1997.

Base Period (1994–1997): In the four years immediately preceding the housing bubble, the index declined at an average annual rate of 0.2% per year, which is roughly consistent with the trends over the previous century.

THE PHASES OF THE BUBBLE

Liftoff (1998–2001): During the four years of Liftoff, housing prices suddenly surged upward, with the index increasing at an average annual rate of 4.7%.

Acceleration (2002–2005): During the Acceleration, the rate of home price appreciation escalated appreciably, to an average annual rate of 8.3%, peaking at 10.4% in 2005.

Deceleration (2006): In 2006, the rate of appreciation suddenly decelerated dramatically, dropping from over 10% in the last year of Acceleration down to "just" 3.5% for the year.

Crash (2007–2012): In 2007, real home prices started a multiyear decline, eventually falling 33% from their peak in 2006.

THE CAUSE OF THE LIFTOFF

The Liftoff of the housing bubble was triggered by the government-sponsored enterprises (GSEs), Fannie Mae and Freddie Mac. First established in 1938, Fannie had been a nonfactor in the national housing markets until, in the late 1960s, its charter was expanded and Freddie was created as a competitor. Structured by Congress as private enterprises in order to move their debt off the federal government's books, the GSEs were also endowed with special privileges that gave Washington a powerful tool to influence the national housing markets. These privileges gave the GSEs competitive advantages that virtually assured that their influence over housing finance would expand during the subsequent decades.

By the late 1990s, the GSEs controlled 40% of national housing finance. This is the first key point missed by so many: for the first time in the nation's history, the specially privileged GSEs had become something of an 800-lb. gorilla with enough heft to move the national housing markets. Beginning in 1998, the GSEs embarked on a massive supply-driven expansion. Combined with their sizable market share, this expansion was sufficient to push housing price appreciation meaningfully above the long-term trend.

In the four-year Base Period preceding the bubble, when housing prices *declined* slightly relative to inflation, the GSEs' combined book of business grew by an average of a little over 7% per year. During the four-year Liftoff phase, when real housing prices suddenly took off, the GSEs' book of business grew by an average of 15% per year. This growth spurt happened suddenly. In the last year of the Base Period (1997), the GSEs' combined book of business grew by about 6%. In the first year of Liftoff (1998), their book of business grew by 16%.

This growth was also unique to the GSEs. Growth in the rest of the mortgage market edged up slightly during Liftoff, but by nowhere near as much as GSE growth increased. The unmatched surge in growth at the GSEs and their declining interest rate spreads provide convincing evidence that the Liftoff was driven by the increased supply of housing funds suddenly gushing forth from these politically privileged institutions.

THE CAUSE OF THE ACCELERATION

Like the GSEs, the Federal Reserve, through its control of short-term interest rates, was also uniquely capable of influencing housing prices on a national basis.

Traditionally, single-family home loans were predominantly long-term, fixed-rate instruments, which tended to match the ownership intentions of homebuyers. Interest rates on these loans were typically higher than the rate of appreciation on the homes themselves. Buyers still financed their home purchases with high levels of leverage because of other factors—tax preferences, avoiding rent payments, lifestyle considerations, etc.—but the historical relationship wherein mortgage interest rates were typically higher than the rates of home appreciation tended to discourage speculative home-buying.

When the Fed dramatically lowered short-term rates in the midst of the rapid escalation of housing prices previously ignited by the GSEs, however, it unwittingly changed these dynamics. Suddenly, homes could be purchased with short-term debt at rates well below the rate of home price appreciation, which created a historically rare opportunity to greatly enhance the equity returns from highly leveraged home purchases. This sparked a demand-driven buying spree that caused home prices to escalate even faster during the Acceleration than had been the case during Liftoff. In turn, this dynamic gave rise to massive demand for adjustable-rate mortgage financing, which Wall Street investment banks (like Bear Stearns and Lehman Brothers) and large commercial banks (like Citigroup and Bank of America) were only too happy to supply.

THE FINANCIAL CRISIS

The housing bubble led to a systemic buildup of mortgage debt relative to GDP, which magnified the risk that problems in the housing markets would spread to the economy as a whole. In the four-year Base Period (1994–1997) preceding the bubble, national home mortgage debt outstanding averaged 44% of GDP, which was roughly equal to the average for the first half of the 1990s. By 2007, home mortgages had grown to 72% of GDP.

This led to systemic holdings of mortgage assets at institutions from across the regulatory spectrum, including the GSEs, large commercial banks, and the major investment banks. When the housing bubble began to collapse in 2007 and home prices continued their downward trend in 2008, it pressured the value of the mortgage assets held by the critical financial institutions, thereby threatening their solvency.

Having watched the authorities at the Fed and the Treasury step in to rescue markets from one potential crisis after another, dating all the way back to the 1987 stock market crash and continuing through the bailouts of Bear Stearns and the GSEs in the first half of 2008, the money market mutual funds and other providers of short-term capital were initially stressed, but not panicked by what was happening. Then, when Lehman was unexpectedly allowed to fail in September 2008, the financial markets panicked.

Systemic exposure to mortgage assets whose values were threatened by the collapse of the housing bubble is why, unlike prior investment banking failures, Lehman's failure provoked a financial panic.

The authorities responded to the panic with a bailout sink of programs. Some of these programs undoubtedly helped, but none calmed the panic readings in either the TED spread or the S&P 500. What the short-term financing markets were looking for was unconditional assurance that none of the remaining critical institutions—Citigroup, Merrill Lynch, or Bank of America—would become the next "Lehman surprise." The final bailout package for these critical institutions was announced in mid-January of 2009. The TED spread almost immediately returned to pre-Panic levels. Shortly thereafter, the S&P 500 bottomed out and then began a sustained recovery.

The stress tests that the Fed conducted on many large financial institutions were released *after* the recovery in the financial markets was well under way. The results of these stress tests confirmed that the financial system as a whole was in generally sound condition, and that the real problems had been limited to a few critical financial institutions, which, by the time of the stress tests, had already been bailed out.

PREVENTING A FUTURE FINANCIAL CRISIS

Without the unsustainable home prices and systemic exposure to mortgage debt resulting from the housing bubble, there would not have been a financial crisis in 2008. Given the understanding of the bubble set forth here, the keys to preventing a similar crisis in the future are relatively straightforward:

1. Eliminate the role of the GSEs in the national housing markets.
2. Eliminate or dramatically curtail the ability of the Federal Reserve to inflate asset bubbles through interest rate policy.
3. Require variable net asset value reporting for *all* money market mutual funds.

RISK MONITORING FOR FINANCIAL INSTITUTIONS

The preceding analysis of the financial crisis suggests some guidelines for boards of directors, executives, and regulators overseeing financial institutions. Rather than (or perhaps in addition to) focusing on arcane and hard-to-evaluate models that purport to show financial strength, such participants should do the following to monitor risk:

1. Measure key underlying areas of asset exposure against historical benchmarks for signs that bubble-like conditions are developing. Robert Shiller's index is an excellent point of reference for housing. Similar standards are readily available or could be developed for other major asset classes.
2. When a significant deviation from past pricing norms develops for an exposed asset class, monitor tangible stockholders' equity (TSE) as a percentage of the investment in the endangered asset class. This means watching this ratio in comparison with past norms and contemporary industry peers.
3. Take steps to ensure that TSE relative to the exposed asset class is within the bounds of pre-bubble norms, is at the high end of the range for industry peers, *and* seems capable of withstanding even a "hundred-year flood" type of event.

THE FEDERAL RESERVE

Straightforward measures that are relatively easy to evaluate can also be highly useful for discerning when Federal Reserve policies are likely to elevate systemic risks. I believe that the real federal funds rate (the difference between the FF rate and current inflation) provides an excellent measure of Federal Reserve policy. After the Fed's runaway inflation from the 1970s had finally been tamed, and prior to the start of the housing bubble, the real FF rate averaged 2.5%. Whenever the real FF rate falls much below this level for an extended period, market participants should be on guard that there is an elevated risk of either high inflation or asset bubbles.

-34-

LESSONS OF HISTORY

POLITICALLY PRIVILEGED INSTITUTIONS

Alexander Hamilton's vision for the United States was built in part on a mercantilist economic model like that of Great Britain, in which the government bestowed privileges on certain private institutions that then worked hand in glove with government to further its objectives. To this end, he established the first Bank of the United States, using the Bank of England's charter as a guide. In contrast, Thomas Jefferson's views were heavily influenced by Adam Smith's belief that government should take a more hands-off approach to economic matters.

Like the first Bank of the United States, the Second Bank of the United States was also a Hamiltonian institution, a privately owned entity endowed with special government privileges. Andrew Jackson believed that the Second Bank used its powers to interfere in elections and had an unhealthy ability to control the economy. After campaigning on this issue and after a prolonged and messy fight with its supporters, Jackson closed the Second Bank. A severe economic downturn followed, but then, under Jefferson's laissez-faire model, came perhaps the greatest prolonged period of growth and upward mobility for all classes in modern history.

The creation of the modern GSEs as private institutions endowed with special government privileges in the late 1960s was very much in the Hamiltonian tradition. Their privileged status enabled the GSEs to gain considerable influence over the politicians who oversaw them, as well as over the housing markets and thus the wider economy. The extraordinary cost associated with the housing bubble and the financial crisis provides another lesson in the dangers of Hamiltonian interventions.

THE FEDERAL RESERVE

The Great Depression of the 1930s and the stagflation of the 1970s both illustrate the dangers of misguided Federal Reserve policies. Reflecting on these episodes, Milton Friedman wrote:

> The System has not made the same mistake that it made in 1929–33—of permitting or fostering a monetary collapse—but it has made the opposite mistake, of fostering an unduly rapid growth in the quantity of money and so promoting inflation. In addition, it has continued, by swinging from one extreme to the other, to produce not only booms but also recessions, some mild, some sharp.
>
> In one respect the System has remained completely consistent throughout. It blames all problems on external influences beyond its control and takes credit for any and all favorable occurrences. It thereby continues to promote the myth that the private economy is unstable, while its behavior continues to document the reality that government today is the major source of economic instability.[1]

Consistent with Friedman's observations, the powers of the Fed were expanded greatly in the aftermath of the financial crisis. Why has the Fed continued to grow in power and influence despite its culpability for each of the major periods of economic distress experienced over the last century?

Despite all protestations to the contrary, the Fed is a highly political institution. The chairmanship of the Fed, an appointment made by the president of the United States, is the most highly prized position in all of economics. Much like a U.S. president, a Fed chairman's success will be measured in large part on whether he or she is reappointed to serve additional terms. In this way, the Fed chairman is beholden to the most powerful political official in the world. Human nature only adds to these political pressures. Just as nearly every aspiring politician wants to someday be president and nearly every aspiring rock band once wanted to be like the Beatles, nearly every Fed chairman wants to be seen as a "maestro"—and none want to be charged with failing to act when they had the power to do so.

And so the chairmen act, and each action tends to expand the mandate of the institution. And when such interventions lead to dysfunction—as they have so many times in the past—that dysfunction is either covered up by additional actions or, as Friedman observed, blamed on the market. Either way, the institution's powers expand further.

All of which was evidenced by the long sequence of events leading up to the crisis of 2008: bailing the Reagan administration out of the potential consequences of the stock market crash of 1987, the Fed's stealth financing of the Long-Term Capital Management rescue in the late 1990s, and the effort to help save the Bush administration from the consequences of the collapsing tech stock bubble by lowering interest rates to a point that inflated the housing bubble that led to the financial crisis.

As evidenced by this period, these actions lead to market expectations that the Fed will step in to bail out an ever-increasing array of participants from an impending crisis. If such expectations are shattered, as when Lehman Brothers was unexpectedly allowed to fail, the markets go into a tailspin... and the Fed responds by bailing out more institutions to keep the tail from spinning further out of control. This then establishes the precedent that the Fed will bail out virtually any "systemically important" institution.

In addition, those institutions deemed systemic, or "too big to fail," have now been endowed with special government privileges. As was the case with the GSEs, the capital markets will treat the systemically important firms more favorably because the risk of loss in a crisis is lower than with firms that lack a federal backstop. Over time, we can expect that the financial system will become increasingly concentrated in the hands of such institutions, which will only elevate the risks to the system, as happened with the GSEs. As we have seen time and again, including with the GSEs, the idea that increased regulations will counterbalance such increased risks to the system is likely to be but a false promise.

Those with an interventionist bent will have a hard time finding fault with these ever-growing expansions of federal control over the system. Those Fed chairmen who start off on the other side of the interventionist divide will find it nearly impossible not to cross that divide once they have risen to the most influential position in all of economics. Those firms that have been deemed systemic and "too big too fail" will find it very difficult to dislike a system that has so favored them relative to their competitors. In spite of the Fed's many failures, these factors endow it with an enormous wealth of political, intellectual, academic and even marketplace support.

And so, to paraphrase the Beatles: When we get to the bottom we go back to the top of the slide where we stop and we turn and we go for a ride till we get to the bottom and we see you again.... Helter skelter.[2]

ACKNOWLEDGMENTS

Thank you to my amazing network of family and friends for supporting me during the many years it took to bring this project to fruition. In addition, I'd like to extend an extra note of gratitude to my dear friends Bill Koehler, who helped inspire the idea of writing this book, and Sean McPartland and Charlie Uhrig, who read and provided helpful comments and encouragement. Special thanks also go to Terry Considine for not only reading the book and offering encouragement but also for introducing it to Roger Kimball and his remarkable team at Encounter Books including: Elizabeth Bachmann, Clare Rahner, Sam Schneider, and Carol Staswick, to name those I've had the pleasure of working with so far. Without your help and support, this would not have come together. Finally, thanks to Nancy Wolff at Cowen DeBaets, Abrahams & Sheppard LLP for your expert legal counsel and advice.

NOTES

PART I—INTRODUCTION
-1-

1 Jon Meacham, *American Lion: Andrew Jackson in the White House* (Random House, 2009), 53.

2 Peter Temin, *The Jacksonian Economy* (W. W. Norton, 1969), 15–16.

3 Ibid.

4 Ibid.

5 Ibid., 26.

-4-

1 Milton Friedman and Rose D. Friedman, *Free to Choose: A Personal Statement* (Harcourt, 1980), 90.

PART II—THE HOUSING BUBBLE
-5-

1 Ron Chernow, *Alexander Hamilton* (Penguin Books, 2004), 43.

2 Jon Meacham, *American Lion: Andrew Jackson in the White House* (Random House, 2009), 53.

3 Richard W. Stevenson, "A Homecoming At Fannie Mae: Franklin Raines Takes Charge Of a Most Political Company," *New York Times*, May 17, 1998.

4 Ibid.

-7-

1 Simon & Garfunkel, "Mrs. Robinson," track 3 on *The Graduate*, Columbia Masterworks, 1968.

-9-

1 Audioslave, "Shape of Things to Come," track 8 on *Revelations*, Epic, Interscope, 2006.

PART III—THE LIFTOFF PHASE OF THE BUBBLE
-10-

1 Congressional Budget Office, "Assessing the Public Costs and Benefits of Fannie Mae and Freddie Mac," May 1, 1996, https://www.cbo.gov/publication/10339.

2 Ibid.

3 Susan Woodward and Robert Hall, "What to do about Fannie Mae and Freddie Mac?" https://woodwardhall.wordpress.com/2009/01/28/what-to-do-about-fannie-mae-and-freddie-mac/, accessed October 26 2023.

4 Congressional Budget Office, "Assessing the Public Costs and Benefits of Fannie Mae and Freddie Mac."

5 Bethany McLean, "The Fall of Fannie Mae," *Fortune*, January 24, 2005, https://money.cnn.com/magazines/fortune/fortune_archive/2005/01/24/8234040/index.htm.

6 Jon Meacham, *American Lion: Andrew Jackson in the White House* (Random House, 2009), 53.

-12-

1 Bob Dylan, "The Times They Are a-Changin,'" track 1 on *The Times They Are a-Changin'*, Columbia, 1965.

PART IV—THE ACCELERATION PHASE OF THE BUBBLE

-14-

1 Lennon-McCartney, The Beatles, "I Am the Walrus," track 6 on *The Magical Mystery Tour* LP, Parlophone (UK)–Capital (US), 1967.

2 Alan Greenspan, *The Age of Turbulence: Adventures in a New World* (Penguin Books, 2007), 24–26.

3 Ibid.

4 Ibid., 30.

5 Ibid.

6 Ibid.

7 Ibid., 40.

8 Ibid., 51.

9 Ibid., 132.

10 Ibid., 138.

-16-

1 Bethany McLean, "The Fall of Fannie Mae," *Fortune*, January 24, 2005, https://money.cnn.com/magazines/fortune/fortune_archive/2005/01/24/8234040/index.htm.

2 Lennon-McCartney, The Beatles, "Drive My Car," track 1 on *Rubber Soul* LP, Parlophone (UK)–Capital (US), 1965.

-17-

1 Ben Bernanke, "On Milton Friedman's Ninetieth Birthday," Remarks by Governor Ben S. Bernanke—At the Conference to Honor Milton Friedman, University of Chicago, November 8, 2002, The Federal Reserve Board, https://www.federalreserve.gov/boarddocs/speeches/2002/20021108/.

2 John B. Taylor, *Getting Off Track: How Government Actions and Interventions Caused, Prolonged, and Worsened the Financial Crisis* (Hoover Institution Press, 2009), 2.

3 Ben S. Bernanke, *The Courage to Act: A Memoir of a Crisis and Its Aftermath* (W. W. Norton, 2015), 91.

PART V—THE FINANCIAL CRISIS

-19-

1 Sarah Bartlett, "Where the Ace Is King," *New York Times Magazine*, June 11, 1989.

2 Julie Won, "Watch the scotch tape expense and don't confuse luck for brains," Hanson + Doremus, September 15, 2021, https://hansondoremus.com/watch-the-scotch-tape-expense-and-dont-confuse-luck-for-brains.

3 Bartlett, "Where the Ace Is King."

4 Won, "Watch the scotch tape expense and don't confuse luck for brains."

5 Doron Levin (Detroit Free Press), "Careful wording of memos can get employees to see things your way," *Orlando Sentinel*, April 10, 1996.

6 Ibid.

7 Ibid.

8 Interview: Alan "Ace" Greenberg, "Inside the Meltdown" series, *Frontline*, PBS, posted February 17, 2009, https://www.pbs.org/wgbh/pages/frontline/meltdown/interviews/greenberg.html.

-20-

1 Lennon-McCartney, The Beatles, "The Long and Winding Road," track 6 on *Let It Be* LP, Apple, 1970.

-24-

1 David Bowie, "Changes," track 1 on *Hunky Dory*, RCA, 1971

-25-

1 Joshua Cooper Ramo, "The Committee to Save the World," *Time*, February 15, 1999.

2 Ibid.

3 Ibid.

4 Roger Lowenstein, *When Genius Failed: The Rise and Fall of Long-Term Capital Management* (Random House, 2000), 222.

5 Ben S. Bernanke, *The Courage to Act: A Memoir of a Crisis and Its Aftermath* (W. W. Norton, 2015), 267.

6 Ibid., 158.

7 Ibid., 260.

8 Ibid., 359.

9 Sheila Bair, *Bull by the Horns: Fighting to Save Main Street from Wall Street and Wall Street from Itself* (Free Press, 2012), 4.

10 Ibid., 6.

11 Ibid.

12 Ibid., 159.

13 George Harrison, The Beatles, "Piggies," track 4, side 2 on *The White Album* LP, Apple, 1968.

14 Bernanke, *The Courage to Act*, 373.

15 Ibid., 374.

16 Ibid., 375.

PART VI—INVESTMENT BANKS, MONEY MARKET FUNDS, AND ALTERNATIVE THEORIES OF CRISIS

-30-

1 David Levy, "Interview with Milton Friedman," Federal Reserve Bank of Minneapolis, June 1, 1992, https://www.minneapolisfed.org/article/1992/interview-with-milton-friedman.

2 Ibid.

3 Jonathan R. Macey, "Reducing Systemic Risk: The Role of Money Market Mutual Funds as Substitutes for Federally Insured Deposits," Yale Law & Economics Research Paper No. 422, January 4, 2011, https://papers.ssrn.com/sol3/papers.cfm?abstract_id=1735008.

4 R. Alton Gilbert, "Requiem for Regulation Q: What It Did and Why It Passed Away," *Economic Research: Federal Reserve Bank of St. Louis*, vol. 68, no. 2 (February 1986), https://research.stlouisfed.org/publications/review/1986/02/01/requiem-for-regulation-q-what-it-did-and-why-it-passed-away/.

5 Marcin Kacperczyk and Philipp Schnabl, "How Safe Are Money Market Funds?" *Quarterly Journal of Economics*, vol. 128, no. 3 (August 2013): 1073–1122, https://www.jstor.org/stable/26372519.

6 Matthew P. Fink, *The Rise of Mutual Funds: An Insider's View* (Oxford University Press, 2008), 84.

7 Macey, "Reducing Systemic Risk."

8 *Report of the President's Working Group on Financial Markets: Money Market Fund Reform Options* (October 2010), 11, available at https://www.sec.gov/files/rules/other/2010/ic-29497.pdf.

-31-

1 Andrew W. Lo, "Reading About the Financial Crisis: A Twenty-One Book Review," *Journal of Economic Literature*, vol. 50. no. 1 (March 2012): 151–78, https://www.jstor.org/stable/23269975.

2 Barry Eichengreen, "Financial crisis: Revisiting the banking rules that died by a thousand small cuts," *Fortune*, January 16, 2015, https://fortune.com/2015/01/16/financial-crisis-bank-regulation.

PART VII—CONCLUSION

-34-

1 Milton Friedman and Rose D. Friedman, *Free to Choose: A Personal Statement* (Harcourt, 1980), 90.

2 Lennon-McCartney, The Beatles, "Helter Skelter," track 6, side 3 on *The White Album* LP, Apple, 1968.

INDEX